A Path to Gratitude
Find Your Enchanted Castle
REFLECTIONS OF AIMEE AND SUSAN

Susan Crockett Touchet & Aimee Young Hopkins

Edited by: Paul Tracey and Andrew Young

2019

Copyright © 2019 by Susan Crockett Touchet
& Aimee Young Hopkins .

ISBN   978-1-970160-72-7   Ebook
ISBN   978-1-970160-73-4   Paperback

All rights reserved. No part of this publication may be reproduced, distributed, or transmitted in any form or by any means, including photocopying, recording, or other electronic or mechanical methods without the prior written permission of the publisher. For permission requests, solicit the publisher via the address below through mail or email with the subject line "Attention: Publication Permission".

EC Publishing LLC
11100 SW 93rd Court Road, Suite 10-215
Ocala, Florida 34481-5188, USA

Ordering Information:
Quantity sales. Special discounts are available on quantity purchases by corporations, associations, and others. For details, contact the publisher at the address above.

www.ecpublishingllc.com
info@ecpublishingllc.com
+1 (352) 234-6201

Printed in the United States of America

ACKNOWLEDGEMENTS

Aimee:

I would like to thank my tremendous family, especially my husband, for allowing me the time to complete this book while raising children and balancing household duties and work. Thank you for being my partner and sharing the load always, ever-supporting my creative visions! Thank you to my girls, who inspire me every day and are in so much of my lists. Thank you to my dear mom, the original wellspring of my creativity, my strong and gentle dad, who is always with me, my precious stepmom and now good friend, my girlfriends who give me the strength I need to carry on and face each challenge, and my amazing mentor, Susan, without whom none of this transformation or project would be possible! Lastly, thank you to amazing Andrew and persistent Paul, our co-editors, who pushed to the last word, letter, page number and typo! THANK YOU!

Susan:

My contribution to this book is dedicated to my kind, loving and wise daughter, Heather. From the moment of her birth, I could see she was a gentle soul, yet strong in character. She has endured many challenges in her life, facing adversity with courage and determination. She is exceptionally fair and just. I wish to thank my husband who flows unconditional love to me. He seems to genuinely like me for who I am - which is amazing! What better gift can one give to another? I also thank my stepchildren for the lessons they have taught me in spite of our differences; they have created fulfilling lives. And, I am especially blessed to have five grandchildren - each unique and exceptional. Thank you to Aimee who trusted my guidance as we traveled the path we agreed to explore. She is truly a blessing! Thank you Paul for your many hours of work and high standards of excellence, and Andrew who bravely came with knowledge and reinforcements to help us produce this book.

CONTENTS

Acknowledgements	
Contents	1
Introduction:	3
A Year Of Gratitudes	6
Who Is Susan?	8
Who Is Aimee?	11
A Sampling Of Daily Gratitudes	16
Steps To Guide You To Write & Share Daily Gratitudes	26
Thoughts On Fear	27
What Is A Code Of Honor?	30
Code Of Honor	31
Code Of Ethics	32
A Selection Of Aimee's Gratitudes	33
Back Story On Designing A 25 Year Plan	36
Ideas For Designing Your Own 1, 5, 10 Or 25 Year Plan	38
Five Year Plan (2015 - 2020)	39
Chart Of Aimee's 5 Year Family Plan	45
Chart Of Aimee's 25 Year Plan	46
Aimee's Advice On Creating A Vision Board:	47
My Vision	48
What Is A Stepdaughter? What Is It Like To Be One?	49
What Is A Stepmother? What Is It Like To Be One?	53
Do I Have Any Advice?	56
Ground Rules	57
Two New Chapters In My Evolving Role	
Ch 1 Gaslighting	59
Ch 2 Death, Dying, and Suicide	60
Helping Aging Parents And Negotiating With Your Stepmother	68
Taking Responsibility For Making "End Of Life" Decisions	70
My Health	73
The Topic Of Criticism	76
Advice On Mentees	82
What Is A God Box?	84
More Gratitudes	85
Unity	93
Epilogue: You Can Engage In A More Joyful Life	94
Prompts	95
List Of Artwork	99

Introduction

What are the healing powers of daily gratitude?
What can happen when you share them with a trusted friend?

Susan:

I was working as Director of Curriculum and Teaching Artist Development at the Music Center: Performing Arts Center of Los Angeles County. Part of my job was to train and mentor our teaching artists, one of whom was Aimee Hopkins - a vocal artist. It was during this period when I got to know her and learn more about her other work - being a mother, a performer and teacher, running a business - and struggling to keep all of the pieces in balance.

When I was about to retire, she asked if I would mentor her outside of my job, and I agreed. She would write to me about challenges she was having. I would listen, ask questions, and give some guidance and support. Then, she began to check in with me periodically, giving me progress updates and reporting things that still troubled her. From time to time we would meet for lunch and dialogue. Some issues persisted and she became anxious as her father, who was divorced from her mother and remarried, became very ill.

Aimee is one of those multi-talented women who has high standards for doing everything well. This was pulling her in too many directions - to be the "perfect" mother to her two young girls, the "perfect" wife, the "perfect" teacher and performing artist. She also started a business that included identifying and training her own roster of teaching artists, as well as finding schools for their work, and taking care of all of the accounting and executive duties.

This was enough of a struggle, but her father, who lived in Alabama, was the straw that almost broke Aimee. She wanted to be there to comfort him, but it required her to leave her family or take them with her; additionally, she felt the pressure of interrupting her work. She was at that stage when one's responsibilities in life become overwhelming. She was exhausted and it became too much for her to keep striving for her "perfect" standards. When she went alone to see her father, she also had to make arrangements with her mother to help her husband care for their daughters. Someone else needed to supervise her business. Then, when she got to Alabama, she had difficulties dealing with her stepmom, and eventually with her father's caretaker.

Something had to give, take less time, change, or be healed. Aimee, being the spiritual woman that she is, picked the option of healing. She began by healing herself and letting go of self-judgment. She slowly realized that she had to let go of some responsibilities, and that it was OK to be a "pretty good" mother or teacher. She knew that she always did her best under the circumstances, even though it might not be "perfect."

I was the one who suggested Aimee might write ten gratitudes every day for a year to help her rebalance her perspective. Unexpectedly, she asked me if I would join her and write ten of my own each day. I thought for a moment, and then accepted her challenge. I never imagined how much focus, intention, discipline and reflection it would require. I did well for the first five days - until I found I was starting to repeat myself. Needing to broaden my awareness and see beyond the obvious things for which I was grateful, I began digging deeper, using microscopic eyes to look under the layers of the life I was taking for granted. As I "awoke," my curiosity increased. I started finding previously hidden gems. Then, Aimee and I began to give each other encouragement - not judgment or evaluation - but cheering each other on to discover more.

Our daily gratitude exchanges helped each of us put a positive spin on anything and everything that was happening in our lives. It was a journey of healing and awakening. It was a journey of self-acceptance. It was a journey of setting healthy boundaries and finding the positive in all situations. Even if Aimee was overwhelmed, she gave gratitude for a good cup of coffee, or reading to her girls at bedtime.

As the weeks and months went by, we discovered that certain situations, issues or themes came up over and over. Writing the daily gratitudes helped us climb out of our ruts. We began to take on specific issues and figure ways to better them. Aimee had a major insight into the role her stepmother played in her father's life. She was able to see the positive things her step-mother did for her Dad. Eventually Aimee changed her own attitude. I guided her at the beginning of this process, but she continued on her own. Being a stepmother myself, I knew what a difficult and mythical role this was. A good friend (also a stepmother) once told me, "One day I am going to rewrite the story of "Cinderella" from the stepmother's point of view!" This new version of the old story was a gift I could share.

I have chosen to take a Nom de Plume rather than using my given name. This is to provide me some cover as I share thoughts that could be upsetting to others in my life. I felt a desire to express my true thoughts and show the steps of processing challenging things. I have selected names from my ancestors that share the same rhythmic pattern as my true name. So, my "nom de plume" is Susan Crockett Touchet.

"Ten Past Toucan"
collage by Susan

"Randolph Rainbows"
Fungus carving by Aimee

A Year Of Gratitudes

Aimee:

In 2006, I had been working for ten years as a Teaching Artist, traveling throughout greater Los Angeles with my own and other arts education companies, when I got a call from Susan Crockett Touchet. She was with the Music Center of Los Angeles, and she made me an offer to receive training to become a high-level Teaching Artist with one of the finest companies in the United States. What an honor!

I was able to take what I had learned through my B.A., Masters, and teaching credential, and gel them into a cohesive teaching methodology which impacted my teaching from that day forward. Plus, I was surrounded by the highest quality of human beings I had ever met. They were out in the field like me, every day, working with children as outside guest artists. I had found my tribe!

After several years of working with the Music Center and with Susan, I found out that she was going to retire. I asked her to be my mentor outside of work. I was feeling a need for more balance. We had had our second child and my dad was ill, it was 2012 and I was now 41. I was having trouble with my voice, teaching and singing so much with large groups. I was struggling to visit my dad and care for him, but cross-country travel was using all extra funds and energy for these trips.

In 2014, I began writing my 10 gratitudes every day, and asked Susan to join me. I was honored that she said yes. We began a daily email dialogue, motivating me and shifting my thinking. What amazed me most was her ability to read through my lists and comment on just what I needed to tweak or notice.

Susan's sharing about being a stepmom herself was the most transformative part of this exercise for me, and perhaps for her. I was able to transcend the role I was playing and to acknowledge my stepmom with the deepest gratitude and forgiveness. I even made amends for my constantly reacting to my stepmother and her choices, choices which, I realized through Susan's help, all grew out of her love for my dad. It was a magnificent spiritual experience on every level.

Susan and I said, "Wow, one day we should put these together into a book!" And so, here we are! We hope you enjoy it almost as much as we have enjoyed this process.

"What Goes Around Comes Around"
collage by Susan

Who Is Susan?

I am finally back to being the person I was at four years old, only now with more life experience - relationships, adventures, losses, gains, and wisdom. I have stripped away most of the traits that are not essential to who I am. Now, I must admit that every moment has been a miracle, even the really difficult ones. I see my life as a collage, with bits and pieces from all aspects coming together in unexpected ways to form a series of unique art works.

I have been blessed to have had inspirational parents, family, friends and teachers. From my earliest memories, I have always believed in, and communicated with God. I knew I was protected by angels - in fact, I felt I was an angel. I was wondering where my wings had gone, and if they would grow back. I used to ask my parents what I was supposed to do now that I was here on earth. They would tell me that it was my job to be a child and to be curious and play, as well as learn the basics.

Perhaps the reason I felt I was an angel was because my paternal grandmother's maiden name was Angell. Her ancestors were among the early Mormon pioneers who made the big trek from Nauvoo, Illinois, to Salt Lake City, Utah. However, when my grandmother was a young wife, her mother (my great grandmother) left the Church and her community because her husband (my great grandfather) was asked to take another wife. My great grandmother left her home and husband and moved in with her daughter; they all burned their undergarments as a final break with the Church. During my childhood there was a lot of conversation between my grandparents and my parents about the Angells - especially my great-great grandfather, Solomon Angell, a builder, and his brother Truman, who was the architect of the Mormon Temple in Salt Lake City. Their sister, Elizabeth, my great-great aunt was the first Mormon wife of Brigham Young - who went on to have 57 wives! This is probably a factor in why my great grandmother rebelled when her husband was asked to take another wife.

Since that event - leaving their faith community - my family didn't attend any church. But, I had a big desire to go to church and learn about God and what my job here would be. I learned about these things from my babysitter, a 13 year old girl named Marie. Eventually, when I was 4 1/2 my parents agreed to walk me to the Episcopal Church at the corner of our palm-lined street in East Los Angeles. I attended Sunday school by myself, dressed up with a hat, purse, gloves and black, patent leather shoes. A few months after I began this ritual, I was asked to be an angel in the Christmas Pageant. I was so excited, until I found out that I was one of 25 little angels. I had expected to be the main angel since I knew that I was a genuine angel. I thought of it as my birthright. My family supported me, but I was disappointed.

This is all background into who I am - I consider myself to be a very spiritual person, but I do not belong to just one religion. I have learned from many groups and faiths. I think there are multiple paths that lead to being an evolved spiritual being. In fact, I would subscribe to what the current Dali Lama said when he announced, "My religion is kindness." So is mine. It is in this vein of thinking that I designed my own "Code of Honor" (explained later in our little book, page 30).

Since I was 14 years old, I have held many different jobs in differing roles, but my deepest desire has always been to empower others to be the best they can be and to give hope, support, justice and opportunities to all. My profession for the past 57 years has been focused on modern and improvisational dance, the arts, and arts education. I have been a high school and studio dance teacher, Director of an all arts pre-school, a dance therapist, a dance artist, a national dance-movement specialist, arts education administrator, writer, film-maker, certified Hatha yoga instructor, daughter, wife, sister, mother, step mother and grandmother.

"Fruit in a Blue Bowl"
by Susan

"We Shared Something"
a collage by Susan

Who Is Aimee?

 As a child in 1st grade, I asked my parents to take me to church. We joined the U.C.C. (United Church of Christ) in our small Rhode Island town, and stayed there for the remainder of our time in that State. I went through Confirmation there when I was 18 and made a covenant to join the church as an adult. This was based on the informed decision of what it was, what it meant, and what I could accomplish there.

I always knew that I was an artist. I always felt connected to nature, God, people and the arts. There was a patch of light in my bedroom where the sun streamed in, with four squares for the panes, and I remember playing, dancing, writing, drawing in that patch of light. It was pure joy for me. I escaped into my own imaginary world there and was never bored.

I drew, painted, and sketched all the time. My family thought I would be a visual artist. The teacher at my elementary school often asked me to walk down to the office and show my work to the principal to hang it up. They put my work in contests and I took classes at Rhode Island School of Design in Providence to learn some more skills.

"Childhood Home"
by Aimee

The neighborhood children used to come over and I would direct them in plays. I made costumes, created scripts, usually fairy tales such as "Little Red Riding Hood."

In high school I wrote a play about autism which won the Henry Fonda Young Playwright's Award and I was rewarded with a staged reading in Providence, Rhode Island. I thrilled at hearing the lines I wrote being said by professional actors. In college I wrote prolifically and performed in my own shows with friends and colleagues. I won the New England Theatre Conference Playwriting Award, seeing my work produced in a staged reading.

In the college dance studio one day, seeing a patch of light, similar to the one in my childhood, I wrote in my journal that I wanted to BE that patch of light for the world. I wanted to shine light into a dark world, especially for women and children. I had already started working at age 11, babysitting, scooping ice cream, painting and prepping wooden furniture for a local woman artist, teaching theatre at the YMCA, and I knew I wanted to help women and children especially through the arts.

After moving to Los Angeles in 1996, I was taking a jog around Los Feliz when I saw a U.C.C. church. I went in, and I have remained there ever since, over 20 years now. My husband and I married there, our children have been baptized there, and my 14-year-old daughter is now going through their Confirmation process. She visits other congregations, studies, enjoys fellowship with other teens, does service projects, and ultimately decides whether or not to join the church at the end of this year.

From age 18 to age 28, I traveled a long road to find the God of my understanding and to come home to Him now. I tried evangelical Christianity, Judaism, self-help, no faith at all, New Age, agnosticism, and more. Now, here I am back at the U.C.C. church where I started!

Full circle! It is important to me to accept all other religions as valid paths up the mountain to God, and to be, not just tolerant, but pluralistic. I value the U.C.C.'s position on women's rights, gay rights, diversity, racial acceptance, and the mission to serve the poor and homeless in our communities and beyond with local and international aid relief.

What a blessing it is to have this peace inside me every day, even when circumstances are tough! I always know that I am not alone and that God's got my back. I know that He is always looking out for my Highest Good. Sometimes things don't look the way I think they should, but if I just let go and relax, pray, meditate, and ask for Divine Direction, God's way is always better than what I could design in my own mind.

Along with my parents and brother, my family participated in church and community service projects. Later, my dad changed his religion slightly when he met my stepmother. He joined the Episcopal church in Alabama. I grew to understand and accept his decision, and to find common ground with both him and my stepmother in this new dimension of spirituality.

"Twilight at the Cafe de la Créativité"
Aimee Hopkins

I consider myself to be a spiritual person. I have learned from many groups and faiths. I think there are many different paths that lead to being an evolved spiritual being. In fact, I would subscribe to what the current Dali Lama said when he announced, "My religion is kindness." So is mine. It is in this vein of thinking that, inspired and encouraged by Susan, I designed my own "Code of Ethics" (explained later in this book, page 32).

Since I was 11 years old, I have held many different jobs and been in many different roles, but my deepest desire has always been to empower others, specifically women and children, to be the best they can be, and to give hope, support, justice and opportunities to all. My strategy to do this has always been through the arts. Starting as a babysitter and entrepreneur in my small town (holding park play-dates with a theatre act for neighborhood children!), and growing into a Theatre Arts Enrichment Instructor at the local elementary schools at age 17, I have always believed that the arts are a road through which I can serve the world and empower others to develop increased self-esteem, literacy, and joy!

I started my own business, Aimee Art Productions: Building Self-Esteem and Literacy Through the Arts, with a business license in 1996, but really I have been doing it all my life. I even made greeting cards for my family as a child and in college, and on the back wrote, "Aimee Art Productions." Now, I see that this is God's plan for me. Right now, it means teaching music, theatre and dance at elementary schools, preschools and in my home studio in Los Angeles. I help other Teaching Artists develop as professionals. We now have 25 employees. We offer affordable arts education services to children, women and families.

And I have come to believe that it is my job every day to be in the moment, present and awake to what God gives me, to embrace this path with my whole heart, to rest and care for myself so that I can be of maximum service to God and others, and to practice spiritual principles above personalities in all my affairs. My other big job is to LET GO! Every day I need to let people be who they are, let others have their opinions about me, let myself be imperfect, and let life happen of it own accord. I walk in faith even when situations look bleak or uncertain. I ask myself, "What does it mean to have faith rather than living in fear? Where is God in this?" I show up for life and bring my best self, and let

God go before me. This is how I bring my faith into the world to the best of my ability.

"Artist Kim's Studio #1"
by Susan

A Sampling Of Daily Gratitudes
10 written daily, 365 days, by Aimee (AH) and Susan (SCT)

AH - Sun. Aug. 10, 2014 at 7:41 AH

To SCT

1) Feeling more settled, caught up and grounded after opening all mail and email and catching up on work
2) Good work day yesterday morning, and the chance to take my kids to see Katelyn play Olivia in 12th Night at Shakespeare in the Park yesterday afternoon - she was great! Show was great, and we got to reunite with the girls' camp friends who live in the area
3) The chance to pick up my mom at the airport on the way home from the beach
4) Good dinner last night with my family
5) Watching a Chipmunks movie with my daughter in a fort we built with pillows, blankets and chairs
6) Feeling pretty ready for the 1st day of school tomorrow, though I'm not ready for homework to start!
7) Coffee
8) Sleep
9) Quiet times in my pajamas, learning to rest
10) Feeling less of a need to interpret the actions of others learning to let go and let it be interpreted how it's meant to be interpreted

SCT - Sun. Aug 10, 2014 at 2:51 PM

Nice ones Aimee. Here are mine.

1) Yoga
2) Former student returning - needing help
3) Still conducting Teacher Workshops
4) Maddy (our "English" daughter) hanging out with us - lying on our bed watching Netflix
5) One more day before grandkids return
6) Seeing kids tonight for dinner
7) Have close friendships with people of all ages

SCT - Wed., Aug. 13, 2014 at 9:26 AM

To AH

Hi Aimee - Your list is a great one. I just saw a series on the History Channel about FDR and all that it took for him to get ready each day for the simplest of tasks - going to the bathroom, getting dressed, sitting, walking a few yards with leg braces - all because he was paralyzed from the waist down. And yet, he led the effort to turn the tide on WWII and made so many important decisions, attended meetings, gave speeches that both uplifted people and tackled large problems - driving or taking trains and never letting people know the effort that daily actions required of him.

I was so awed at his ability to keep his strong and positive attitude, not feel sorry for himself, and fulfill his life's purpose. I don't think I can ever feel that any limitations or challenges I have can hold me back from giving my all. As my father used to say, when he was in his late 80s - "Susan, you must keep going at your best level with whatever you've got left!" So, I am glad you are confronting your "doubting thoughts."

Love, Susan

AH - Wed 13, 2014 at 10:05 AM

To SCT

Thx Susan - this is such a great reminder. Thx so much!

"Artist Kim Studio #2"
by Susan

AH - Sat., Aug 16, 2014 at 7:15 AM

To SCT

Hi Susan! Hope you're well and the MC (Music Center) stuff is going well this week, enjoy this beautiful day!

1) A good night's rest
2) Getting me and my girls through the first week of school successfully, and on time (always a miracle for me)
3) A fun girls' shopping trip last night for tap shoes, school shoes, backpack, school and office supplies, Starbucks, and then home for hot tub and dinner

4) Bring soup to another mom who was sick and taking her kid for her for 5 hours and a "half-sleepover" (dinner, bath and pajamas, then home to sleep)
5) Doing really well with difficult personalities at work, keeping it soooo simple, thank you S, R and M.
6) Light and polite is a beautiful thing
7) A wonderful new client this week where I'll go once a week all year long, and guess what's across the street? Baskin Robbins!!! A new habit for a special treat
8) Meeting today and a good, easy work day ahead which includes my kids, exercise and a lot of fun, and took a dance class for me to take - just for me
9) Things are working out with my schedule so far and I'm finding pockets to rest and rejuvenate
10) Deep restorative sleep!

"Under My Hat"
by Susan

"Shared Dreams"
collage by Susan

SCT - Sat. Aug. 16, 2014 at 4:42 PM

To AH

Hi - I especially love #4 and #6. Here are mine.

1) Yoga
2) Teaching a lovely group
3) Getting all ready to make our second movie with grandkids.
4) Inviting another child to join our cast - empowering her "Eagles vs Peacocks"

5) Getting all costumes ready. Seeing Paul create a very innovative costume that requires him being a peacock who tries to impersonate an eagle in our little movie
6) Getting every scene organized, all cooperating and successful.
7) So far, no confrontations with my SD
8) Finding an imaginative way to find a role for Sarah in our video.
9) Watching Hugh play tennis in a local, Pacific Palisades tournament - and, then win!!

"Sunset with Beach Grass"
by Aimee

AH - Aug. 18, 2014 at 8:40 AM
To SCT

1) "Feelings are not facts" - I can feel crappy today and know it will pass; it's not my whole life or my state of being, no judgment
2) I do feel a little better today after lots of rest.

3) I can turn over my tooth extraction to the higher wisdom of the universe
4) I can let go of decisions that were made in my absence and trust that the greater good will is done in the group conscience
5) I got to walk my kids to school today
6) My kids are safely ensconced in school and I can focus on work, and I will see them at school today since that's one of the places I work!
7) I get to pick up my younger daughter at the gate today and take her with me to my other job and meet my husband there
8) I can rest tonight
9) I have a lot of flexibility and time off with my work, more than many people, though it's hard to be self-employed sometimes; I'm grateful for the flexibility and autonomy

"Jealousy Has A Long Red Tongue"
by Susan

SCT - Tues, Aug. 19, 2014 at 7:35 AM

To AH

Sounds like you are deepening and getting more comfortable with a more healthy, balanced life. I traveled yesterday so my gratitudes are all around my family.

1) Having Skylar (my grand-daughter) to create with
2) Having the trust and new-found love and trust with Hugh (my grand-son)
3) Zach (my grandson) running full out to greet me when he spotted me at the airport
4) A nice, easy talk with my daughter Heather after Zach went to bed and before Pablo and Finn got home
5) Zach insisting on sleeping with me!
6) H and P (my daughter and son-in-law) giving me their bed and top of the line jacuzzi bathroom
7) Feeling loved and appreciated by my four grandchildren

8) Deciding with Hugh and Skylar that we would say, "to be continued . . . "rather than "good-bye" when it was time to return to their home in England. (future possibilities rather than sadness.)
9) Seeing my daughter and son-in-law loving toward each other and with their children
10) Knowing Paul will join me in a couple of days

AH - Tues, Aug. 19, 2014 at 8:18 AM
To AH

Thx Susan. I sooooooooo enjoyed your movie. (Original scripted movies with grandchildren) Wrote you separately, but holy creativity!

SCT - Wed. Aug. 20, 2014 at 7:28 PM
To AH

1) Waking up with one of my grandsons snuggled up next to me!
2) Heather's friends inviting me to go with them to Chesapeake Bay
3) Spending all day with 2 lovely women and 5 boys
4) Being at the Atlantic Ocean
5) Seeing my daughter happy and easy
6) Again, seeing the high quality of my daughter's friends
7) Zach asking again to sleep with me
8) Zach playing "Frère Jacque" on the Kalimba
9) Knowing how special all I am experiencing is
10) My health

AH - Thurs. Aug. 21, 2014 at 7:03 AM
To SCT

1) Extra sleep
2) Coffee
3) My mother-in-law and my mom reading to the kids last night so I could wrap up my work and we could all get to bed and still have time to snuggle, correct homework and read more
4) Finally figuring out Dropbox, not as hard as I thought

5) Adding water pic and nasal rinse to my am routine - not glamorous but helping my overall health
6) Good doctors, dentists and healers
7) A good work day yesterday, letting go is everything
8) My business is actually doing better since I let go and eased up a little bit
9) My amazing bookkeeper
10) My mother-in-law here making breakfast and getting the kids to school so I can go to work in peace without stress

AH - Sat. Aug. 23rd, 2014 at 9:17 AM

To SCT

1) Making a choice to rest this am before teaching and to take my time
2) A delicious "Rhode Island dinner" in the yard last night by the fire (clam cakes, chowder, grape nut pudding) - my "home cooking" from my original home

Vision Board
by Aimee

3) Picking up my daughter at gym last night, having time together.
4) My daughters' teachers are both happy to have volunteers in the classroom this year, which is fun for me
5) Dance recital with preschoolers this morning will be fun
6) Making cookies this afternoon for my nephews and getting a present for my sister-in-law with my girls
7) Looking forward to spending the day at my brother's pool tomorrow and celebrating with them
8) A great first rehearsal yesterday with students
9) Getting a few outreach calls from friends yesterday really helped my day
10) Planning trip with my brother to see my dad next weekend, open to the adventure

AH - Sun, Aug. 24, at 2014 at 8:19 AM

To SCT

1) Just because I feel crappy sometimes doesn't always mean I'm doing something wrong, need more self-improvement, etc. - sometimes I just feel crappy - but reading and writing this am did help too
2) Remembering HALT (hungry, angry, lonely, tired) can help so many things
3) Some quiet time alone with my husband this morning before anyone woke up
4) Finally sitting down and drafting a rough 25 year plan with my husband (open to higher wisdom's plans for us, of course!) which we've been meaning to do for a while now
5) My mentor! So wise . . . so generous
6) My mentees who call me and email and text me and remind me of what's really important
7) My source who has given me, my husband, our kids, our home, our jobs, our cars, all of this was not my doing
8) Getting help and keeping things simple - I'm not the spring chicken I used to be and need to take it slow with work stuff

9) Someone called me a "force of nature" in the kitchen and multitasking - I realize now that most forces of nature move slowly, deeply, powerfully (ocean, wind, weather patterns)
10) Recitals went well yesterday and good work and play day

* 25 year plan is explained later, page 46

SCT To AH

Lots of good insights - love the one about "force of nature." Love, Susan

Steps To Guide You
To Write & Share Daily Gratitudes

Step #1 - Make a commitment to share 365 days of gratitude, uninterrupted.

Step #2 - Identify key topics and issues you struggle with.

Step #3 - Dig through your day and write things you hadn't really noticed before. You will discover many gifts.

Step #4 - Validate each other every day for finding new things to be grateful for. Avoid giving advice or judgments.

Step #5 - Ask questions, rather than give answers. Be both the student and the teacher.

Step #6 - Examine your life with a more positive spin - Write guiding principles known as "A Code of Honor." *

* Code of Honor is explained later, page 31

"Ravine House Raft"
by Aimee

Thoughts On Fear

Gratitude is the antidote

Aimee:

I have come to believe that gratitude is the antidote for fear. Because I am so sensitive and have an active imagination, I have many fears and sometimes have trouble detaching from them. I used to be afraid of being homeless; now I feel confident that I would do whatever it takes to support myself and my children so that this would never happen, and that if it ever did, I would still be taken care of.

Two years ago, my brain developed a fear of going to jail. I know why; it is a childhood fear. I don't like when someone is mad at me and I do not like enclosed spaces. What I have learned is that my God will protect me from whatever life throws at me, and that this fear is really just a way of my brain giving me adrenaline so that I can scare myself into pushing myself more. This is a technique my brain learned as a child, to overachieve. I no longer need this fear. I have given it to my Higher Power, and I continue to do so every day. I know that (a) this is an irrational fear (b) that anxiety lies, exaggerates, and "catastrophizes" and that (c) my brain developed a strategy for my ego to stay alive, creating a fear of the one thing it knew it couldn't survive, which is going to jail. My ego no longer rules me now, as I have conquered this fear with gratitude. To this, I say, "No!" I erase that thought with goodness and fill the space with love and gratitude. When each new thing comes up in my business around legal and financial matters, I ask God for help and I say, "Just for today, I let love come to my aid." I also tell myself out loud, "I graciously accept good into my life, and all my needs are abundantly met, now and always."

The more I learn about the brain, the more I also see that this is the oldest, deepest, reptilian part of my brain, the "fight or flight" part. And that, though it is still a part of me, it is not needed. I can say, "Aimee, you have choices. Your choice is less in the external, and more in your attitude, and in how you respond and not react. Pause, breathe, and respond with love and gratitude." This saves me every time. And when I forget, and when I react, I don't always like the results, but through the grace of my Higher Power, the lessons are not painful. I can say, "Oh well!" and move on. No one is hurt in the process and the damage is usually minimal, because I am aware and I seek counsel right away when I don't know the answer. I know that I am never alone. I have the support of my family, my community, my friends, Susan, and my God.

Marianne Williamson* states, "Our deepest fear is not that we are inadequate. Our deepest fear is that we are powerful beyond measure. It is our light, not our darkness that most frightens us. We ask ourselves, who am I to be brilliant, gorgeous, talented, fabulous? Actually, who are you not to be? You are a child of God. Your playing small does not serve the world. There is nothing enlightened about shrinking so that other people won't feel insecure around you."

*Marianne Williamson, from A Return To Love: Reflections On the Principles of A Course in Miracles

"The Divine Feminine"
by Aimee

A Wonderful Thought

We are all meant to shine, as children do. We were born to make manifest the glory of God that is within us. It's not just in some of us; it's in everyone. And, as we let our own light shine, we unconsciously give other people permission to do the same. As we are liberated from our own fear, our presence automatically liberates others.

What Is A Code Of Honor?

Susan:

A Code of Honor is a name I chose for developing standards for thinking, doing and being the best person I can be. They are drawn from core beliefs I learned from my parents, grandparents, teachers and spiritual guides.

I keep this posted on a mirrored closet door in my office. I check it from time to time, especially if I have had a difficult day or am in conflict. It helps ensure that I follow "True North" rather than veering off to "Magnetic North" - which can often lead me astray.

"Joy"
by Susan

"Determined Pachyderm
Heading West"
by Susan

Code Of Honor

Susan

I will:

Do my very best in all things. Live each day fully
~
Not waste time doubting myself or my choices –
I know I did the best I was capable of at the time
~
Be respectful and kind to all people;
greet them with love, light and compassion.
Do good actions in the world
~
Have clear, viable, ethical principles at the foundation of my life
~
Detach from feelings of shame, guilt and fear
imposed on me by myself or others
~
Live without judgement of self or others
~
Strive for justice, equity, access, and equality for all people.
I will speak up for people who need my support
~
Be true to my family and support them,
even when they don't understand my actions
~
Respect the environment and my community
with the least negative impact possible
~
Care for my body and my mind, making healthy choices
~
Forgive myself when I fall short of these principles

Code Of Ethics

Aimee
I will:

Be kind to all people I encounter and greet all with love,
light and compassion

Do good works,
not necessarily always being "nice" out doing good actions in the world

Put principles before personalities,
and not necessarily be friends with all.
I will work together with compassion
and get the job done with excellence

Leave shame, guilt and fear at the door
and ask for spiritual help to remove these one day at a time

Do my best work to the best of my ability
without judgement of self or others

Not waste time doubting myself or my choices –
I know I did the best I could at the time

Not do for others while they can do for themselves,
or what they haven't asked me to do

Not knowingly allow injustice to occur
when there is a clear action that I can take against it

I will care for myself and my family before I care for others

Respect the environment and my community
with the least negative impact possible
and with gentle acts of preservation when possible
(i.e. conservation, donations, tithing, service)

Do my part to protect children and the elderly,
people with disabilities
and those who cannot speak for themselves, when appropriate

Teach with best practices without wearing myself out,
using my energy efficiently
and with the highest level of effectiveness possible in each situation,
serving the population with whom I work

Stand up for the rights of myself, my family,
and others when appropriate and necessary

"View from Mountain Porch"
by Aimee

A Selection Of Aimee's Gratitudes

AH - Mon. Aug. 25, 2014 at 7:03 AM

To SCT

1) Learning to ask, "Where is the spiritual lesson or higher wisdom in this?"

2) Hearing my friend's voice in my head saying, "I think you're forgetting Good Orderly Direction in this," oh yeah, when I don't see how I can do it, God can help me when I ask, and always does. . .

3) Meditation even for short times. My will was to stay inside and get things done yesterday, apparently the higher wisdom's will was to get me out to play in the water, and I still got a lot done before, during, by the pool, and after, so I'm ready for the week

4) Finances are fine - there is enough, just for today

5) My kind, hard-working and good-attitude husband

AH - Tues, Aug. 26, 2014 at 7:15 AM
To SCT

1) One day at a Time
2) Making a decision and turning it over; when obsession and doubt crept in, I was able to put it down like a drink - progress
3) The "priceless gift of serenity" - ok to spend the money to take something off my plate and to stay in a hotel with family visits when necessary
4) "Be as a child" - I finally understand this for myself, keeping things more simple so I can be happy, joyous and feel like a child. I don't have to complicate things so much just b/c I'm an adult now
5) Adjusting my attitude toward visiting my dad this weekend, open to the possibility of getting closer to my brother and dad, and maybe even D (stepmother)
6) Accepting what is, not fighting it so much or thinking something is wrong

SCT - Tues, Aug. 26, 22014 at 7:20 PM
To AH

Hi Aimee,

Sounds like progress. I just read two amazing articles on the plane today - one on hopefulness and one on forgiveness. I will make copies for you. Just got home and finished taking a yoga class - a bit hard, but feel good that I did it. I did look at your 25 year plan, but I think it would be best to discuss it over the phone when you return. Basically, I looked at it from the point of view of balance in the different parts of your life, remembering that "less is more." This means that rather than scattering your energy in so many directions, it would be best to select a few aspects to target and develop them more fully. It is the concept of either an inch deep and a mile wide or a mile deep and an inch wide. Of course, these are two extremes, but it is good to think of balance, spaces, time to recuperate and time together with your family without stress.

"Sunflower Tea"
by Susan

Back Story On Designing A 25 Year Plan

Susan:

> "Begin doing what you want to do now.
> We are not living in eternity.
> We have only this moment,
> Sparkling like a star in our hand -
> And melting like a snowflake."
>
> Sir Francis Bacon

This idea of "A 25 Year Plan" came about the year before I would become 50 years old. I decided to do an assessment of my life, including what I had accomplished during my adult years.

By the time I turned 49, I had married for a second time and added two stepchildren to my family of two children, making us a group of six. I had many accomplishments in my career as a dance movement specialist and arts education administrator, and had recently survived a major tragedy - the sudden death of my 19 year old daughter. It had taken me two years to move through the first difficult stages of grief. My progress on this journey was made possible because of the support of family and friends, and a spiritual practice.

One morning during this 49th year, I re-emerged from the darkness and began to see the dawning of my future. I realized how precious and unpredictable life is - and, I didn't want to mourn the past any longer. I wanted to find forgiveness and healing. When I arrived at my new beginning, I found the following quote:

> "Everything that has a beginning has an ending.
> Come to terms with that
> And all will be well."
>
> The Buddha

This quote had been in existence for at least two and a half thousand years, but I discovered it only when I was ready for its wisdom - this is called synergy. This ancient thought became the genesis of "The 25 Year Plan for My Life." My plan was designed to go from age 50 to 75, taking me to the fulfillment of dreams, repairs of relationships and targeting my efforts toward empowering me to focus on my life's purpose. As I write this, I am 78 years old and have succeeded in fulfilling my 25 year plan, plus so much more than I could have imagined. In my 25th year, as I reviewed my plan, I decided I would write a new 5 year plan to guide me from 75 to 80. And, if I am so fortunate as to still be here, I will determine whether I will write another 5 year plan, or perhaps a 1-3 year one. These plans are a way to guide my actions to fully realize my life.

One additional note is that a good friend of mine, Melinda Williams, told her boss, Joan Boyett, that I was writing a 25 year plan. Her boss asked her to invite me to bring it to a conference we were all attending in a few weeks. When we arrived at the conference, Joan asked if I would share my plan and vision with her; after I did, she decided that she wanted me on her creative team. So, a few weeks later I was offered a great job in arts education that last lasted me 25 years . . . and is continuing still.

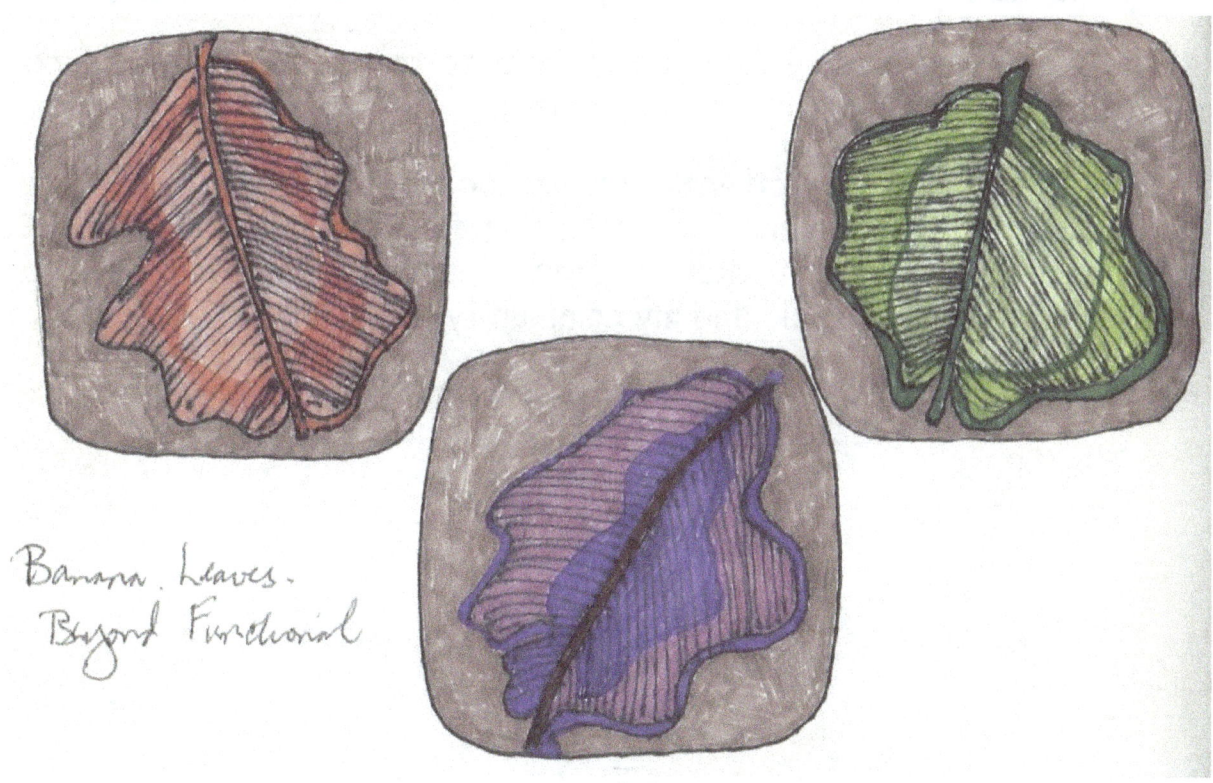

Banana Leaves.
Beyond Functional

by Susan

Ideas For Designing Your Own 1, 5, 10 Or 25 Year Plan

Look at it from different perspectives: this could include such things as:

- **Self** - what can I do to improve my own mental, physical, spiritual well-being?

- **Family** - this can include a partner, children, friends and relatives - How do I improve and contribute to the lives of those closest to me?

- **Community and Work** - What can I do to fulfill my purpose and also contribute to others through my work or community?

- **My Surroundings and the Things I Own** - How can I better respond to the needs of my house, car, things, shared things such as fences?

- **The Natural World** - How can I contribute to maintaining a balance in nature, conservation, my carbon footprint.

- **World of the Arts, Self-expression, Aesthetics** - beauty, inspiration, problem solving in a practical and aesthetic way. How can I contribute to these creative and aesthetic aspects of life and develop these things within myself and my community?

- Find a connection to the **Rest of the Universe**

"Bumpy Car Ride to Cashel & Tipperary"
by Susan

Five Year Plan (2015 - 2020)

Susan:

1. **Taking Care of Myself**
   - Keep up the patterns of care I already do (hair, nails, etc.)
   - Add flossing and mouthwash 1-2 times daily
   - Add drinking greens and/or roots once a day - also smoothies
   - Make a daily decision to bring love, compassion, forgiveness and my best effort
   - Continue to do yoga 6 times a week - 5 is acceptable
   - Pilates 2 times a week
   - Sleep with thoughts of peace and kindness to myself - get enough rest every night
   - Plan a trip to Europe to see some of the sites where Medieval ancestors lived

- Accept opportunities to do workshops, talks, leadership roles in areas I know
- One thing leads to another. Have clear intentions and then trust the process
- Trust and follow my intuition in all things

2A. My Relationship with Paul (my husband of 37 years) - My top Priority!

- Show my genuine love for him in all things
- Be considerate to him in all ways
- Listen to him and respect his ideas
- Greet him with love every morning; don't go to bed angry; or agree to rest and then tackle difficult decisions or problems
- Make decisions that are mutually agreeable on all things
- Make our relationship the most important thing - we must keep our union clean, ethical, supportive, and nourished - and not let others try to come between us
- Make full use of our beautiful garden and studio
- Celebrate each other's victories in life. Be there for each other's challenges

2B. My Relationships with all of our Children and Grandchildren

- Give each offspring our best support and encouragement, but don't solve their challenges in life for them. The goal is to make them strong, competent and able to handle whatever happens in their lives. Know that we are not their future - each must meet their future without us. We are models, advisors and cheerleaders

"Squared Spirals"
by Susan

- Keep what needs to be private - private, but avoid having family secrets about important things. Trust that others can work through relationships if they wish and if both are emotionally competent to do so. Don't interfere
- Be loving and supportive of my family members
- Continue to make gifts to the arts /worthy causes in Julie's name
- Do all that I can to contribute to their lives without taking over or allowing them to be dependent on us, emotionally or financially
- Fully research my ancestors and organize it all for the family

**"Yin and Yang
a Constant Struggle for Balance"**
by Susan

3. **Groups I am a part of - Work I do with Community - Ways I Contribute**

   - Continue to work to support the Music Center for as long as I am needed
   - Continue to find work as a facilitator
   - Continue to find ways to contribute to Arts Education
   - Continue to build yoga classes
   - Continue to grow and develop as a yoga teacher, weaving in spiritual aspects
   - Continue to work with privates, adapting work to meet individual needs
   - Strive to make a minimum of $1,000/week to supplement my SS and retirement
   - Continue to feature exceptional people and their stories at salons every 2-3 months. Ideally 4 per year

4. **Contributions to All of Mankind**

- Be more cognizant of ways to assist the environment (recycling, solar power, less water, less garbage, etc.)
- Continue to use my spiritual energy to put good thoughts into the world
- Continue to stand up to bullying, people crossing boundaries; intimidators; manipulators and people with low ethical behavior. Stand firm, or be strong and grounded when needed. Don't be afraid of standing up for, or stating, things that need to be said - things that benefit the whole
- Financially support organizations/individuals who are working for good
- Stand up for those who cannot stand up for themselves; support civil rights and the right of all people to have a happy, productive life and participate in opportunities to make that happen
- Support health care, fair wages, food, lodging, education, opportunities and respect for all people

"Lupe's Mother's Day Gift"
by Susan

5. **Contributions to All Living Things**

- Be kind and protective to animals and the natural world (plants, trees, ocean)
- Take time once a week to work in our garden to care for our plants, and do weeding
- Support Paul in making contributions to the natural world. He is best at this

6. **Contributions to the Physical Universe**
   - Assess our house and work in phases to make updates, unified and in good condition for the next 25 years. My goal here is to clean, design, build, and lessen the clutter so that as we grow older we will have a delightful interior and exterior; will not need to do this when we have little income and are perhaps physically weaker
   - Continue to keep my car in good shape
   - Continue to clean out my closets of unused clothes, shoes, etc.; buy only pieces I need. I have enough - remember this!!! The spiritual path involves letting go

7. **Contributions to Personal Expression and the Arts - Spiritual Plane**
   - Continue to create in every aspect of my life
   - Find specific art forms - jewelry; collage; explore drawing and painting; revisit the ukulele or piano
   - Revisit my Creativity piece and find a time to share/perform it - complete this project (I did)
   - Support creative people who need financial support

8. **Connection to the larger, greater aspects of life, our universe and beyond**
   - Continue to let go of my ego and seeing myself as separate - know that I am connected to all things in this universe. Open my mind and spirit to connect more fully
   - Refrain from needing to promote my beliefs to others, to refute their beliefs - and to realize more fully that each of us is on our own path. We have different assignments in this life, different karma to balance, different lessons to learn, different people to forgive and release ourselves from

Note: These 8 Dynamics are drawn from the study of Dianetics by L. Ron Hubbard

Chart Of Aimee's 5 Year Family Plan

	Summer 2014	Summer 2015	Summer 2016	Summer 2017	Summer 2018
Aimee	Same	Same	Same	Same	Same
Husband	Same, Sp. Ed, Autism Class	Same Research PhD programs	Same Teach in Sp. Ed	Same	Same
Daughter 1	4th gr.	5th gr.	6th gr.	7th gr.	8th gr.
Daughter 2	1st gr.	2nd gr.	3rd gr.	4th gr.	5th gr.
Mom	Various Free rent	Various Free rent	Various Free rent	Various Free rent	Various Free Rent
Mother-in-Law	Weds. $_____/mo	Weds. $_____/mo	Weds. $_____/mo	Weds. $_____/mo	Weds. $_____/mo
Purchases	Aimee computer Husband laptop	Girls' laptops			Aimee Car
Savings	Aimee SEP Aimee Roth Husband 403B Soc. Resp. Inv. Daughters 529 ($_____/mo) Cash Savings $_____	Same Cash Savings $_____	Same Cash Savings $_____	Same Cash Savings $_____	Same Cash Savings Total $_____
Long-term home	Yr. Cost $_____	Yr. Cost $_____	Yr. Cost $_____	Yr. Cost $_____	Same

Chart Of Aimee's 25 Year Plan

	Spiritual	Financial	Family	Volunteer
2014	Family Group – 16 yrs Bus. Owners' Group – 14 yrs Travel	AAP LAUSD A – Savings $_____ C – Savings $_____	A – 43 C – 44 M – 9 C – 6	School, church, Family Group and Business Group, softball for C
2019	New York Washington, DC			
2022	College tours		M – college C – HS	
2024	Family Group – 26 yrs Business Owner's Group – 24 yrs Church Paris	AAP – studio LAUSD A – Savings $_____ C – Savings $_____	A – 53 C – 54 M – 19 C – 16	High School Church Family Group Business Group Softball Perform? Community Theatre?
2034	Family Group – 36 yrs Business Owner's Group – 34 yrs	AAP C – CSUN A – Savings $_____ C – Savings $_____	A – 63 C – 64 M – 29 C – 26	Family Group Business Group Grassroots Travel? Perform?
2039	Family Group – 41 yrs Business Owner's Group – 39 yrs	Sell AAP? Retirement? Music Ctr? C – Consult? A – Savings $_____ C – Savings $_____ Apt. in Glendale Long summer in NH	A – 68 C – 69 M – 34 C – 31	Family Group Business Group Grassroots Travel?

Aimee's Advice On Creating A Vision Board

One tool that my husband and I have used over the years is a Vision Board. There are many ways to create one, but I have always just sat down with a bunch of magazines, and, without thinking too much, just followed my intuition and cut out images which spoke to me, not necessarily even knowing why. Then, I have glued them onto a board and created a collage of images which feel like what I want in my life. Almost inevitably, these things have materialized for me, sometimes in ways I did not imagine, but which held to the deeper desire.

For example, I put an image of our home on the board, thinking we would one day buy this home or a similar one. We continue to rent our lovely two-bedroom home in a canyon in Glendale, right near the hiking trails, with a gorgeous garden that my husband has built from scratch. We have a hot tub, a trampoline, a guest house where my mom lives, and a wonderful zero-scaped front lawn with a patch of beach sand, which my husband built with a grant from the city to save water. Our rent is low, and our landlady desires us to stay here a long time, and so do we. We have been here 14 years! We love it and we have an amazing lifestyle here. We feel comfortable and safe. The vision has come true, even though we don't own the home!

Another example is when I created flyers for my business and glued them on, and images of how I wanted my business to look. Though I do not have my own brick-and-mortar studio yet, I continue to offer arts lessons in my small home studio and throughout the city. Within our home, my office has expanded to take up more than half of the living room, so we have gotten rid of two couches, and the area around the piano has been cleared so that I can teach a lesson on any instrument or give dance privates here on the wood floor! We also have a small patch of wooden dance floor outside in our garden for me and the girls! It is not exactly the "studio" I imagined, but it is! And one day, I may have an actual place I rent. For now, this flows well with motherhood and finances, and works for all of us!

I have many other examples, but I suggest that you try your own Vision Board and see what manifests! Here is another sample of mine.

Another Example of a Vision Board
Aimee

My Vision

Aimee:

I earn abundantly through my creativity, vitality, and God-given talents, with balance and time for self, family, health and spirituality.

I believe it is important to say this vision out loud at least once a week, and to have another person "hold this vision" for me, as I hold hers. Right now I have an "action buddy" and we bookend actions with each other each week, toward our vision. It is a lovely exercise, and knowing the details of another's life and work is very sustaining as we quietly move toward our dreams and goals.

I recommend this method to anyone who is trying to change aspects of their lives, seek more balance, or struggling to achieve something which they doubt might be possible, as it requires a change in thinking or deeply held old beliefs. For me, these negative beliefs such as "you can't have what you want," "you won't make enough money," or "it has to be hard," are beginning to change as I work toward my vision with my buddy and with my mentor, Susan. What a gift!

"The Tree that Blooms"
by Susan

What Is A Stepdaughter? What Is It Like To Be One?

Aimee:

The role of stepdaughter is a challenging one. I began to be a stepdaughter in 1997 when my father got remarried to my stepmom. I was happy for my dad and liked my stepmom immediately when they started dating. The years from 1997 to 2004 were happy times, getting together for holidays with my dad and stepmom and sharing life, as my brother and I got married, had children, and grew our families and careers.

When my dad had a stroke and got pneumonia in the hospital in 2004, circumstances became much more challenging. My perception at the time was that sometimes my stepmother was controlling my dad's environment, what he ate and how he talked. I now see that she was not controlling and simply was guiding and supporting him. It felt strange to see my dad in the old family house that my grandparents had kept, and how my stepmother was now comfortable and "in charge" in the kitchen there, the way my mom used to be. She was making financial, health, lifestyle and end-of-life decisions with my dad. I now see that this was necessary and appropriate and that she had my dad's best interests at heart.

My visits to Alabama became more frequent as Dad couldn't travel much anymore. I had intense and mixed feelings about my stepmom at that time - both love and distrust. I wanted to care for my dad myself, but moving to Alabama was not a realistic option, nor was it practical for them to move to Los Angeles. When I visited them, I helped my stepmom to prepare meals and give him baths, to change him, help him do his exercises, and eat. I stayed with my dad overnight to give her a break.

My family wondered if my dad should be in a board-and-care or assisted living. We decided that staying in their home was the best option, both financially and for my dad's comfort. I struggled internally as my dad became less able to converse. My stepmom became a conduit to my dad - his eyes, ears, and voice. I was committed to the process.

Sometimes my dad would have bad falls, and I began to feel concerned, unsure of my role and when to talk to doctors, discuss his diet and medications, and know more about my stepmom and dad's finances and emergency plans.

In 2014, I had an internal transformation, due to Susan's help. Susan shared with me how challenging it was to be a stepmom, and to gain the trust of her husband's children. She asked if I had ever written my stepmom a letter of deep gratitude for her tender care of my dad. It slowly began to dawn on me that my stepmom had been the glue which had held my dad together for 12 years. Without her, my brother and I would have had to either move to Alabama or bring him out to California into one of our homes or into a board-and-care or assisted living. I saw the care that my stepmother put into my dad, and how, in our arguments, I had been taking situations personally. Her fastidiousness with cleanliness was to keep germs from his sensitive body, and her adherence to the strict diet was to prevent him from further setbacks. I began to "see the light."

I wrote my stepmom that letter of deepest gratitude and apologized for how I had overreacted. I made amends to her in person later and knew just the words to say and how to say it gently. It was as though the floodgates opened, and my stepmother began to trust me, and I her. Toward the end of my dad's life, my stepmom said, "We're just going to have to trust each other." I made a decision to do so.

Little by little, my stepmom began to confide in me more, and I in her. The last chapter from 2012 to 2016 was about connection with my stepmom and the two of us walking my dad to the other side of life. I had the feeling that Dad was holding on to life until he knew my stepmom and I were connected, and together we would help him cross over into heaven.

I went to see him in August of 2016, knowing it might be for the last time. Over the weekend of his death, I was on a church retreat with my family in the mountains of California. In a circle around his bed in their living room, my dad and stepmother were surrounded by their church community; I was surrounded by mine in a huge circle of love. My stepmother and I thanked God for the cross-country hug with two very different church communities at the same divine time.

My stepmom, brother and I held the funeral together. I went back a few weeks later to go through my dad's things and rest with my stepmom. A year later we had a wonderful memorial near the beach with extended family.

My stepmom and I share our lives on a regular basis, with phone calls, emails, cards, gifts and texts. If it weren't for Susan, I am not sure that I would have made the transformation I had with my stepmom, nor the peace I now feel. I know my grief over my dad would have been so much harder and more complicated if I had not reached a place of surrender, forgiveness and gratitude with my stepmom, and I would not have been able to move forward in my life the way I have. My stepmother is now one of my best friends. Thank you, Susan, thank you to my stepmom, and thank you, God!

"Laguna Beach"
by Susan

What Is A Stepmother?
What Is It Like To Be One?

Susan:

The role of stepmother is perhaps the most hated archetype featured in our human stories. This character role comes with thousands of years of baggage, although the personality of each person in the role has many variations. The characteristics attributed to stepmothers are universal. These include adjectives like: cruel, jealous, selfish, depraved, impossibly vicious, scheming and thoroughly hateful, clever — wicked and manipulative.

Who in their right mind, except perhaps an actor, would audition for such a potentially dramatic role?

Well, I not only auditioned for the role - I was chosen for the part. I gladly entered this new story with high expectations. I anticipated the joy of having a larger family. I looked forward to co-parenting with my new husband, a playful man who is a musician, storyteller, gardener and beautiful being. It seemed to both of us that we had the right ingredients to make this a "happily ever after" story! All of the children were beautiful with great possibilities.

Well, it soon became clear to me that this was not a good

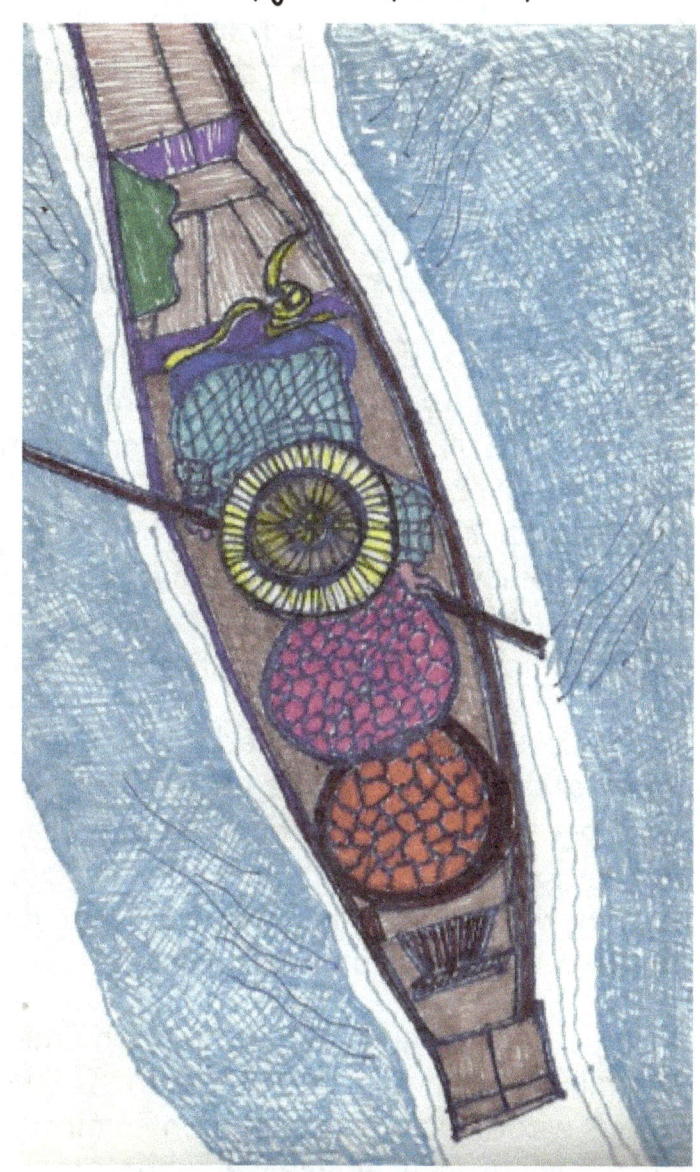

"Floating Market, Thailand"
by Susan

role for me. Family dinners were a time when high drama was played out. One of my stepchildren pretended that the rest of us were not present. He spoke only to his father. The other one chose this moment to start a fight with someone else, resulting in her being asked to leave the table until she could sit in peace with all of us. We tried to hold easy going family discussions to set some ground rules for behavior and responsibilities. We were met with strong resistance - defiance!

Most women who accept this role come with fairy dust sprinkled over their eyes. We want to believe that "Love conquers all." Right? Wrong! Actually, love becomes a thing to fight over. It represents power and control. Stepchildren and stepmothers are forced into this ancient, recurring battle. Who is most loved? Who will survive? In most cases, we all lose; nobody wins. We carry on, but with some form of resentment and sadness in our hearts.

I celebrate those stepmothers who are successful! Brava!

Most people experience me as a kind, compassionate and loving person. My life's purpose is to empower children and teens through the arts. I see children as our future; 57 years of my life have been devoted to being an advocate for inclusion, respect, love and support. I seek to provide opportunities for growth, personal expression and responsibility. When I fell in love with a man who was raising two young children alone, both he and I could see my potential as his wife and parenting partner. However, his children did not share this vision.

Their beautiful and talented mother had become mentally unstable and drove off the cliff at the end of their street, killing herself. They were present when this happened, so they were deeply traumatized by this major event. Their lives changed abruptly and the loss of a beloved mother was shattering. They kept her place in the family alive - there was "No Vacancy" for another mother!

After a year of grieving, my husband met me through the recommendations of two different friends. We were married in a joyous wedding that focused on coming together. Our intention was to form a new family where we supported each other. We all tried very hard. I believe that everyone did their very best under the circumstances of their trauma, different ages, perspectives and personalities. But, nothing we tried seemed to work. My two biological children were shocked and confused being in a hostile and unstable atmosphere. We never did become a family unit. There seemed to be a need - a desire - for separateness, especially on the part of his two children.

I didn't realize that I and my two daughters were seen as invaders and disruptors to their reduced family of three. His two children saw themselves (along with their father and departed mother) as the "true family;" we were perceived as the "false family." After all of our best efforts over 37 years, we have still not been able to heal the rift between the two groups. And, to make matters much worse - early on - my oldest daughter was killed in an automobile accident - renewing the loss, grief, fear and anger in his children. They saw us as bringing more disaster into their shell-shocked world. The separation grew wider and deeper. My youngest daughter was isolated even more. The small threads of healing that had begun were violently ripped apart.

Our family is composed of different groups who do not communicate with each other. We all continue to exist, including five grandchildren, as separate groups. And, quite amazingly, each person is leading a successful life of their own design. We do separate things and have separate celebrations with each of our children. We have a series of unique experiences with each one - our goal is to be "separate, but equal." However, our actions are not always seen that way. There is still jealousy of our time spent with the others.

So, with this experience under my belt, I was able to listen to Aimee and her frustrations with her stepmother - the distrust and the feeling of competition and control in supporting her ailing father. I was given the opportunity to show her the difficulties in the role of stepmother. And, Aimee - being a compassionate and loving person - found a way to reach through the spikes and let her stepmother know that she was seen, accepted and appreciated. It was the beginning of a break-through for both of them to develop a friendship that continues even after her father passed away.

"Red & Green Leaves"
by Susan

Do I Have Any Advice?

Susan:

Yes! After listening to the wisdom of others, and engaging in a spiritual practice of my own, my advice is this:

1. Be kind. Give love even when you don't feel like it. No one can lessen your ability to be kind and loving unless you agree - and with-hold it.

2. Have your eyes wide open. Blow the fairy dust off your eyes; see the reality of what you are either committing to, or a situation you find yourself in.

3. Realize that combining families is a second choice in most cases. The ideal choice is for the original mother and father stay together to raise their children. Most children long for their original parents to remain.

4. It is what it is. Everyone is doing the best they can under the circumstances of what was, what is, and what they think will happen in the future.

5. Don't judge anyone. You can't possibly know what they are thinking or experiencing. Don't project your feelings or interpretation onto them. But, do set boundaries to protect yourself from resentment, anger, shame, blame and curses.
6. Take it one day at a time. Smile, offer greetings and give genuine compliments, rather than finding fault. Focus on what is right - not what is wrong.
7. Take some time to try and see things from the perspective of each person in your "new family unit."
8. Realize that many things that are said to you are "projections" - don't take things personally. Projection is a form of defense in which unwanted feelings are displaced onto another person, where they then appear as a threat from the external world. A common form of projection occurs when an individual, threatened by his own angry feelings, accuses another of harboring anger.
9. Treat all people the way you would like to be treated.

Ground Rules

In offering this advice, it is also important to set some boundaries or "ground rules." Be firm, but not emotional. Neither yelling nor crying are ever helpful. Don't allow people to speak to you disrespectfully. Don't allow others to treat you disrespectfully. Stand up for yourself - let people know when they are going too far. Use a strong and steady voice - but not one filled with anger and hostility. As Eleanor Roosevelt said, "People cannot lessen you without your agreement."

Suggested Ground Rules

1. Greet each other with respect.
2. Be kind.
3. Include everyone at the dinner table. Don't exclude anyone.
4. Begin a practice of identifying 3-5 things you are grateful for each day. Write them down. Share them with your family.

5. Find ways to help other family members. Encouragement is appreciated.

6. Listen without judgment. Encourage everyone to share something about their day, but don't force them. Don't interpret it.

7. Practice the art of Forgiveness. A famous saying is, "To not forgive is like drinking a cup of poison and expecting the other person to die." Forgiving someone does not mean letting him/her off the hook. You are letting yourself off the hook by releasing your need to remain angry and tangled in a hurt. Remaining stuck can monopolize the real estate in your brain and dim your joy. Forgiveness brings freedom. When you can't, or won't forgive, you will be bound by negative thoughts to this person - forever!

8. Genuinely smile and look people in the eye. In yoga, the phrase, "Namaste" means "From the light within me, I salute (greet) the light within you." Focus on the light you see in other family members rather than the clouds and darkness hovering there.

"Create Beauty"
by Susan

Two New Chapters In My Evolving Role

One: Gaslighting

Susan:

Recently, I experienced another series of explosions from my step-daughter - rather, my husband got the fallout from the explosions, which were all aimed at me - but driven through him. They came seemingly out of the blue. We could not spot the event that might have triggered them. However, after being shell-shocked for a couple of days, I had an epiphany. Here it is:

I am very clear that my step-daughter is having a long, enduring tantrum (almost for 50 years). She is like a volcano that shows little activity on the surface, but is burning and boiling deep underground. When she gets insecure, anxious or feels needy, she explodes into a series of major eruptions. When this happens she tries to scare, impress and destroy me with her anger. Sometimes her dad is included in her anger, blaming us both. These major outbursts are meant to make her the controlling force in our universe.

What I believe she is doing in acting out so badly is to see if we will abandon her because we find her unlovable. Seeing her need so clearly has completely calmed me. She is trying to impose a false reality on us. It is often called "gaslighting" - the art of confusing someone with a false narrative. I think the only way to handle these attacks is to stay calmly steady and let the person know that we won't agree to be treated badly. She must also know that we will continue to love her in spite of her horrendous behavior and hurtful verbal attacks. However, she must also realize that the positive aspects of our life-time relationship will suffer - potentially beyond the possibility of repair.

I think some people feel unworthy or devalued. They try to push away those who love them, and yet want to see if we will stay. Her recent behavior took me back to the tantrums I had when I was 3-5 years old. I can remember yelling, kicking and screaming, while keeping one eye open to see how my parents would react to my behavior - and seeing how far I could go before I might push them away forever. Many of us had childhood tantrums. Unfortunately, this behavior sometimes continues as a way to control, overwhelm, and punish those around us. It prevents us from having mature, meaningful relationships.

For victims of this fury, it sets up a situation where we might still love them, but don't want to be controlled, blamed, shamed or bullied. We can only sustain an active relationship with them in small doses. The step-parent often becomes the target for the projected, unhandled emotions and unhappiness they still hold on to from childhood. The only workable antidote I have seen is to know who you are, and stay true to the values you hold. No matter how another tries to manipulate you into being seen as the bad parent in the play they wrote, don't accept that role - and, tell them the costume doesn't fit!

"Kauai #1"
by Susan

Two: Death, Dying and Suicide

This is a letter I wrote to my step-son in response to his asking for advice on how to help his girl friend recover from the loss of her brother to suicide. It's important to know that we have not had an in-depth conversation on any serious topic for over 35 years. Yet, I am the one to whom he reached out for advice.

LETTER 1. - My response to a written request from him to me.

Hi! Thanks for your Christmas wishes.

In response to your question about how to support your girlfriend as she recovers from the loss of her brother to suicide, here are a few thoughts. As she navigates this very emotionally difficult loss - shared with her parents and other family members - these are some ideas that might guide you in supporting them.

1. Each person deals with grief in different ways and it takes varying amounts of time to move through these strongest of emotions - shock - grief - loss - sadness - fear - anger - even a deep withdrawal from life. Sometimes people will feel guilty that the person committed suicide and feel that they could have/should have done more. But, it is not their fault. Suicide is a very desperate action that someone takes when they have a break with living - and have lost hope. They certainly don't realize how much they are also impacting - in a profound way - the people they leave behind. It is a very self-absorbing emotion and action - and often is caused by some form of severe emotional disturbance or even mental illness. So, she and her parents might be feeling some guilt and replaying his life in their minds to re-examine what they could have done differently. This is like having a loop of memories and possible new solutions going around in one's brain - and, often a person needs counseling or guidance to break the cycle and move on.

2. People who are grieving often need space and quiet. It is difficult to allow other people into your world when you are "bleeding inside." If a person can let you in, you do best by being gentle and quiet with them. LISTEN - LISTEN WITH COMPASSION. Don't try to give them advice. Don't try to give them easy fixes. BE VERY PATIENT. Sometimes, just touch them gently - touch their hand - but also know that sometimes they don't want to be touched. Grieving is usually a very lonely process. It requires an extra amount of rest. Calming music, meditation, a walk in nature, or sitting in a beautiful spot can help show them the bigger picture of life again. It is very hard to be happy, join

in fun, or party. A deeply grieving person usually turns inward and seals other people out. It is very hard to not take this personally.

"Life Cycles"
by Susan

3. Your Uncle Jamil met Jenny a few weeks after her finance, John, died from a heart attack - he was recovering from a heart operation in their apartment at the time. One evening, soon after he arrived back home, she heard strange sounds from their loft where he was resting. She ran up to see what was happening and he died immediately. Jenny told Jamil that she couldn't have a relationship with him because she was still grieving deeply. Jamil went into a very tender, kind, loving,

supportive mode and won her heart through compassion, gentleness and by inviting her to talk about John. It helped her a lot for him to sit with her for hours listening to her tell him about John and what she felt in his loss. He made her feel very protected and understood. He gave her a chance to recall her relationship, tell stories of their lives together, talk about his heart attack and his recovery - then, him dying when they thought he was healing and "out of the woods." She built deep trust in Jamil and felt understood and supported by him. The painful ending of one relationship actually led her into the trusting space of a new one. Theirs is a great and enduring love story.

4. So, I might suggest that the key ideas to reconnect with someone who has pushed you away as they grieve are: BE GENTLE AND KIND - SPEAK SOFTLY - LISTEN WITHOUT GIVING ADVICE - BUT PERHAPS ASK QUESTIONS TO ENCOURAGE THEM TO SHARE MORE IF THEY WISH. The hardest thing is not to judge them, try to push them to get over their grief, or give your own thoughts on what they should do. The person is actually dealing with the cycle of life and death and trying to come to some understanding about it as it connects to their own life and other relationships. The person has been deeply wounded and is in a serious healing and recovery process. Perhaps some of this might be helpful to you. I hope so. Love, Susan

Six months later, I received an acknowledgement that was full of appreciation. He wrote and told me that he had applied many of my suggestions and had even developed a heightened awareness about what to do, trusting his intuition.

"Hundred Acre Cove"
by Aimee

LETTER 2. - This is part of the email I wrote back after he responded to Letter #1 six months later.

What a lovely gift to receive your email. I am happy that some of my thoughts connected with you and gave you support. It is all a process, and the feelings of loss and happiness can co-mingle or quickly shift from one to the other. Grieving continues, and I support your insights about what to do. For example, it is very sensitive of you to let her bring up the topic, or stories, or questions about her brother. Your most effective role is to listen, give her a sounding board and every once in a while repeat or paraphrase her thoughts to assure her that you are understanding - lots and lots of listening without judgment, suggestions or interpretations. And, you are right about selecting movies that don't include suicide - no need to re-stimulate sensitive emotional buttons.

So, here are a couple of additional thoughts I will share.

We just attended two memorials last week - one for a dear friend who had the debilitating disease known as ALS, and one for a woman who had an inoperable brain tumor. What one realizes when you attend a funeral or memorial is that these ceremonies are really for the people left behind - not so much for the one who has already left. At each event, people arrived feeling sad and were at different phases of grieving, but at the end each person left somewhat uplifted.

One was a Buddhist ceremony which involved a great deal of strong chanting and lasted about 2 1/2 hours. Their philosophy is that to understand how to live, one must first learn about death and what it represents - loss, change, new beginnings, overcoming one's own fear about no longer being alive in one's body. So, much of their words focused on coming to understand death and what it represents. In the case of the woman, she died slowly over three years, progressively deteriorating. Her family suffered greatly as they watched this once vibrant red-head lose her abilities to walk, write, talk and participate fully in living. The one thing she could do until the end was to chant this one important chant! Their Buddhist philosophy gave them comfort and solace.

In the case of our other friend, it was also a very sad ending for such a vibrant man - ALS is a deterioration of the nervous system and again a three year decline, suddenly ending when he took himself off the breathing machine. At his memorial, his life was celebrated and many friends spoke - but the loss in the lives of his wife, sons and close friends will be painful for some time to come. He was of the belief that he was not his body, but rather a spiritual entity living in his body, much like we use our cars.

So, getting back to the Buddhist philosophy; when one fully comes to terms with death, it can have a strong impact on the way each person chooses to live. Once someone really understands how precious and unique each life is, he or she doesn't want to waste a minute - for death can come quickly, as a shock. Or, it can be a slow process of aging that is natural or from illness that is unnatural. In other words, no one knows what will bring about their death, nor when it will be - unless of course, one chooses suicide. Suicide can seem like a way out of suffering - but it also has a devastating impact on all of those left behind. These "chosen deaths" take a long time to process for families, and many people never get to the point where they can ever be at peace with it. That can very much be the battle that your girlfriend's mother is waging.

"Aging"
by Susan

Suicide is completely unexpected and, in addition, it is completely unnatural for a child to die before their parents. The parent's job is to launch the child into the future. When that future is slammed shut, the parent feels incomplete and somehow unworthy because she/he didn't protect their child (even though an adult). Most parents live with guilt and self-judgment that they didn't do enough to protect their child. It is a terrible burden to carry.

People close to the ones grieving the most can lovingly support those suffering so deeply, but they cannot heal them or save them from chronic sadness. It sounds as if your girlfriend has been quite successful in helping her mother through this dark journey, but her mother must find the will, courage and determination to come to terms with what has happened. She also cannot rely on her daughter to be with her in an enabling role. Hopefully she will come to understand that each adult person is responsible for his or her own life and the happiness or sadness they create. It is a journey that must be walked alone and the gifts tucked into the pockets of the grim reaper require courage, curiosity and determination to find.

However, it is not all bad - for this process can also bring about enlightenment and acceptance for this mysterious adventure we call life. Even if one believes in rebirth, one will

"Greeting Each Moment"
collage by Susan

never again have this life - the life we are in now, nor be with the companions we currently befriend. It is all temporary. There is the NOW, but not necessarily a future.

Love and support, Susan

Helping Aging Parents And Negotiating With Your Stepmother

Aimee:

AH - Sat. Aug. 30, 2014 at 5:36 PM To SCT

1) I'm so glad to be here with my brother - he makes it so much easier and better - he has a great sense of humor
2) Safe and good flight to Alabama and a good night's sleep
3) Good day flying with my brother yesterday - he is so chill and lets me be me, gives me space. We don't always have to talk
4) Doing it differently - getting a caregiver some of the time is really helping all of us
5) Time with my dad, looking at pics of the kids, sharing 40+ years of memories. Taking my dad to buy new shoes with my brother, waiting out a rain shower so Dad didn't get soaked
6) It's none of my business what my stepmother D says about me behind my back - I assume the good in all
7) I have 2 legs and a brain that tells me how to walk
8) I can eat anything I want
9) The beautiful thunderstorms on and off all day

love, peace, Aimee.

AH - Sun, Aug. 31, 2014 at 1:19 PM
To SCT

1) Ability to wake up early and go on a little less sleep
2) Time with dad and brother
3) "Hike" with Dad and brother into a woodsy, rocky area, like we did as kids together - in a wheelchair this time

4) Gratitude for caregiver, helping her, and paying her generously without rescuing her from her car drama - not being a doormat.
5) A long walk by myself
6) Working phone, computer, car and email
7) My health and my family's health
8) Plenty of work booked when I get home and getting a little done here
9) Though I miss my kids and husband, it's also nice to reconnect with myself without kids around me, and I don't have the same separation anxiety I used to have - they are fine without me and have their own path

Love, peace, Aimee

AH - Tues, Sept 2, 2014 at 6:01 AM To SCT

1) Learning to do something nice for myself every day.
2) My "happy list" of things I like to do - I can always go back to that when it feels like drudgery
3) Time with my family by the fire pit last night, and snuggling and books for bedtime
4) My little one coming into our bed in the middle of the night, as usual - a treat I missed for 3 nights
5) You and your lists

love, peace, Aimee

**SCT - Tues, Sept. 2, 2014 at 6:44 PM
To AH**

Good lists Aimee. Yes, it really helps to do these gratitudes together - keeps it fun and steady. Thank you, as well!

1) Yoga
2) Paul seems like his emotional load is lighter now that we have made all of the important "End of Life" Decisions
3) Feeling less judgmental toward family members - know everyone wants to be happy and is doing their best with their circumstances

Taking Responsibility For Making "End Of Life" Decisions

Susan:

Another topic that arose in our exchange of gratitudes was the question of making "End of Life Decisions." Aimee came up against this during her father's illness. These decisions became a challenge that had to be negotiated between Aimee and her stepmother. Who had the greater right to make these decisions? And, was the father able to participate or not? Does the daughter or son have priority, or does the spouse? By the way, there is no "right answer." It can vary from case to case. Values, beliefs, religious traditions, and choices about burial or cremation can also factor in strongly.

This is why it is essential that parents take responsibility for making these decisions before they are incapacitated. When they are not in place, it sets up a potential minefield of emotional confrontation between the key players - who are often left to fight it out. It is a critical factor in breaking up families, leaving them feeling hurt, angry and isolated. Ask yourself the question, "Do you want these to be your final gifts?"

I was fortunate that my parents made these decisions themselves. My father was a judge until he died at 89. He had seen the devastation caused when people left these major decisions "up for interpretation." He was honored because he had successfully guided over 1,000 settlement cases during his career. He would point out to both parties in a case how much lasting damage they would cause when their private matters were revealed to the public. He applied this philosophy to his own life. My parents made their plans together. They didn't get our approval. They remained the responsible people they were. They didn't manipulate us by using their decisions, or their will, as a tool to control our lives. Then, they went about the task of arranging their own burial and funeral - including putting money aside to cover the costs. Of course, it is upsetting to discuss decisions related to leaving this plane of existence - the journey of life into death. Everyone wants to think that they will be the lucky one who avoids this part of the cycle. My advice, however, is to face it, accept responsibility for making your own choices, and then do it!

Buddha said it well, "Everything that has a beginning has an ending. Come to terms with this and all will be well." Yes, it is the coming to terms with death - and accepting the reality that all of us will conclude our lives while the mystery of life continues. People have different beliefs about this transition. These are best honored when the person most likely to die will be courageous enough to make these important decisions, either alone or with their closest ally - someone who knows and respects their beliefs and decisions to end life gracefully, rather than leaving a messy situation for those left behind. And, death can happen quite unexpectedly, as it did for my daughter - so, everyone needs an exit plan.

Taking responsibility to meet with a lawyer or go to a place like "LegalZoom.com," an on-line resource, one can see what choices are available and how to proceed. Consider making a "Living Will" which includes medical and life support issues. Of course, property and money should also be lawfully written out, and this is also possible to do with help from the Internet. In fact, even though I come from a line of lawyers and judges, I bought a book that guided me in how to get my own divorce - and, it worked out well and with fairness - and much less costly than paying lawyers!

In the case of my husband and me, we are a stepfamily with children who don't have a relationship as adults. So, we have made arrangements to have our carefully thought out decisions legally protected. The Executor will not be one of our children, or another family member, but rather a professional connected to a bank, and working with our estate lawyer.

I know that everyone doesn't necessarily want to spend the money required to do this. We made the decision that it was the most important gift we could give to our children and grandchildren. We tried to anticipate every challenge or disagreement that might arise. So, we put in the will's instructions that if anyone challenges any of our final decisions, they will receive one warning to desist. If it continues, they will immediately be removed from receiving any of the estate; their share would be divided among the others. It is called "tough love"

- but, it protects everyone equally. And, being fair and equal is what we hope to model. Once this is all planned and certified, you might be surprised at how free you feel - each day is a beautiful gift to experience, or share with family and friends. A burden has been lifted.

As we both approach our 80s, Paul and I feel free of these decisions. A great weight is lifted. We made these decisions when we were both sound in mind and body. And, we are free to enjoy, not worry about our daily lives and future adventures. However, it shouldn't ever be too late to handle these things before confrontational decisions destroy a family.

"The Tree of Insight"
by Susan

My Health

Aimee:

During the time that Susan and I were writing daily gratitudes in 2014, I was gradually developing what I later found out was a vocal cord hemorrhage. I was starting to have a hoarse voice, and certain areas of my vocal slide were missing around the "break" between my head voice and chest voice. In the "mix," no sound would come out. I went to several doctors. One told me it was acid reflux and to make dietary changes and take some medicine. Another said it might be a polyp or node or nodule. Finally, my own doctor at Kaiser discovered through a scope that it was a hemorrhage. I looked into surgery, but did not want to do it. It was risky and since I was no longer singing professionally but mostly teaching, my goals were not necessarily full vocal recovery as much as overall health.

I began vocal therapy both at Kaiser and at Cedars Osborne Head Neck and Throat Institute, and my life was transformed through these amazing healers. I began to grow in ways I did not expect. I did not speak for what began as 1 week, then turned into 2, 3 and 4 weeks! I walked around with a whiteboard and hired assistants to be "my voice" and teach for me, while I wrote on the board and guided the instruction. It was a miracle. I never missed one day of work! I started sleeping more, resting more, changing my diet and being more gentle with myself. Then, I had to re-learn how to speak properly, and later how to sing. I did vocal exercises every day, which I still do now. My whole life changed.

Then, in 2016, I hurt my foot getting out of the car to teach. It was a bad sprain. I could not teach dance for 4 weeks. I had an assistant teach for me; I iced, elevated, rested and healed.

Then, in 2017, I had a bad cold and fever, went to the doc, and they told me I had high blood pressure! I got a cuff, took my pressure for 3 weeks, worried a lot, changed my diet, and finally decided to go on a low dose of blood pressure medication. I also started working with a homeopath and learned about holistic health. This has changed my life dramatically.

"Aimee Self-Portrait in Paris"
by Aimee

Seeing my dad go "off the grid" with his health and move toward a holistic approach had a big effect on me. I have always been someone who could "eat whatever she wanted," and have never been heavy. However, as I grow older, I can feel the sensitivity of my body, especially to certain foods, and I know that I must listen to that or suffer the consequences. I also saw the impact of the steroids on my dad's overall health, and being on medication for the rest of my life is not something I would choose to do. Therefore, my goal is not to have to take any medication ultimately, if possible. Of course, I surrender to God and will do whatever is needed for me to thrive and be a great mom, wife, business owner and person and to function at my highest in the world.

Now, as 2019 begins, I am on less than half the low dose of the medication, I meditate twice a day with my feet in the dirt, I take barefoot hikes to lower my adrenaline and connect with the earth almost every day, I swim, dance, sleep 8-9 hours per night, and have given up wheat, sugar, salt, and dairy. My asthma has cleared up, my itchy arms are no longer itchy (turned out to be yeast!), my voice is in full swing with all notes of my vocal slide intact, my foot is fine, I feel rested and full of energy most of the time, my anxiety has gone WAY down since giving up sugar, and my blood pressure is perfect! I have not used my asthma inhalers, taken an Ibuprofen or Tylenol or Advil or any other medication in almost a year! Natural health feels so good. I am so grateful that I was able to make these changes with the support of a homeopath, and knowing that Susan has walked a similar path to full health herself.

This knowledge gives me the support I need to continue my regimen daily, and to not take on more than I can handle at any one time. I know that if I do, my blood pressure will go up, my voice will get hoarse, and I will feel anxiety again. I will not compromise on this high level of self-care, no matter how much my family or work demands of me. I have learned to say no, and I continue to learn how to do that with each new scenario. I seek my Higher Power's guidance one day at a time, and pray for discernment in all situations to bring my Higher Self to the situation so that my health is not affected. I pray that I can continue to thrive so that I can live to see my children grow up and have children of their own. Some of this includes not letting my brain tell me that something is wrong or needs to be fixed when everything is really fine. Some of it includes being assertive on the inside, setting boundaries within myself for what I can and can't, or will and won't do. When someone asks, I say "No," or "Let me get back to you." It's much easier and I don't have to get mad, take on too much, or blame the other person when I overdo it.

What a gift! I am so grateful for this health transformation, and I encourage everyone to listen to their bodies and to open up to the body/mind/spirit connection from which everything flows!

"New Hampshire Sunset"
Fungus carving by Aimee

The Topic Of Criticism

Gratitudes by Aimee and Susan

AH - Wed. Aug,. 27 2014 at 9:38 AM
To SCT

1) Being able to shake off criticism yesterday from 2 sources and know I'm doing the best I can. I'm not perfect and that's ok. I'm good enough
2) Being a good enough mom is also good enough for me love, Aimee.

SCT - Aug. 27, 2014 at 10:36 PM
To AH

Hi Aimee,
Who are the people who criticize you? And, what relationship do they have to you? Perhaps you need to set boundaries with them. Tell them that you are not open to critiques without an invitation right now. Or, say, "Thank you for your suggestions. I know they are given with love and respect." Or say, "Good things to consider - thank you" (then, change the subject). Basically, people should not feel that they have a role, or right, or authority to criticize you. They do it to show power or authority or a fight. You need to let them know that this is no longer required, needed by you, or acceptable. This should not be happening, so take a look at why people feel they can do this to you. You are a fully operating adult, mom, wife and colleague.

"Barrington Harbor"
by Aimee, age 9

AH - Thurs, Aug. 28, 2014 at 6:22 AM
To SCT

Hi Susan! Thank you for this! Here is the background on who is criticizing me. One person was a parent at one of my schools who felt the parents should have been informed of Chorus auditions. Some children chose not to audition, but this mom wanted her son to do it, and if she had known, I guess she would have made him. Anyway, long story, but it's a tradition at this school to do the Chorus in 3rd gr., and all 2nd graders know it, and I go to every classroom and explain slowly what it is. I also meet with each teacher to carefully select 5 children and 2 alternates from every class, based on talent, behavior, work habits, self-esteem and other needs/benefits to them. But I talked to the principal and we decided that next year, to cover our bases, I will draft a letter which the office will copy and send home with every child, introducing myself and telling when the Chorus auditions are and explaining my program.

The parent was really upset and I spent probably 30 mins on the phone with her. I didn't know honestly if the main office had already sent something out telling about the auditions, as they tell about all the other activities the first week of school, so the fact that no parents knew was also news to me. So, like many things, it is now back on me, the teacher, to inform people.

I can deal with that. But it's not easy to talk an irate parent down. I did give her child a chance to audition for alternate, and he didn't show up, but mom says he got picked up by dad and would try next week. Teacher says he isn't well behaved in class and shouldn't be in Chorus anyway - he won't be able to leave the classroom and keep up with his work.

The 2nd person was the coordinator of a Performing Arts Ctr. who said there were concerns last fall about the first class (8:15 am) not starting on time and being shorter than the others. She said to let her know if a teacher is late. I said certainly I will be there early this time, and I honestly don't remember ever starting the class late, or if a teacher was ever late (perhaps due to morning assembly). My guess is that she was simply passing on info. I know being early and on time is something I've always struggled with, and it's harder now with 2 kids to get ready in the morning, but I have done really well the last 3 years, and I'm not sure why anyone mentioned it, except that it's possible there was a day when I was still hanging up my posters as they entered or something, as last fall was my vocal cord injury and I needed extra sleep. However, I'm not perfect, and it's something I have to always be vigilant about - allowing plenty of time to get places.

So, maybe criticism wasn't the right word, but I did feel shame when I got the email about being on time, as it means someone had said something "bad" about me, and also talking to the parent made me wonder if I was doing things right.

Hope that helps. Will send my list! I like your suggestion of setting boundaries. My email reply was simply, "Yes, I'll be early and let you know if a teacher is late." And to the parent I just explained the procedure, but I was not a doormat. Love, Aimee.

"Creative Light Bulb"
by Susan

AH - Fri, Aug. 29, 2014 at 6:02 PM To SCT

Thx Susan. Let me know if you had any thoughts about criticisms I got after reading my response yesterday - whenever you have a chance. My brother and I are in Houston boarding a flight to Alabama to see dad. Thanks and love, Aimee.

SCT - Sat, Aug. 30, 2014 at 8:10 AM
To AH

Aimee, my basic instinct is that for being the generous, thoughtful and compassionate person you are, you seem to be around people who feel they have a license to give you critiques. This should not be happening. You are a mature person who is already assessing yourself on a regular basis. For others to place themselves in a role to criticize you is inappropriate. Perhaps you allow this to happen, by feeling you need correction, or giving off an energy that invites people to put you down.

Take a look at what you might be doing that gives others the sense that they have a right to assess you and your behavior. You are way past the point where this should be happening. When this happens, don't react, but rather look directly at the person and simply say something like "OK." Then, change the subject or walk away. They seem to be using criticism to have some power or control over you - or to lessen, weaken, or make you feel less powerful. Think of the criticism as being more about them than about you. Have a lovely time. Sending you loving thoughts. Susan

AH - Sat. Aug. 30, 2014 at 8:44 AM
To SCT

Thank you Susan. I appreciate this very much. One of the critiques was in the context of work with Santa Clarita from my supervisor, so not sure if you got to read that email but I can resend if you like. In a way, that is her role - so I tried to just say, "OK." Like you said. Anyway, I was curious as to your feedback on that specifically, but in general I think you are correct and this is really something for me to look at. I think I have the ability to be even happier than I already am by deflecting criticism or shining it off in a healthy way. Love and gratitude, Aimee.

SCT - Sat. Aug. 30, 2014 at 4:59 PM
To AH

Yes, some critiques are helpful and allow us to change and grow. Other critiques are a manipulative attempt to lessen us. XxoS

AH - Sat. Aug. 31, 2014 at 8:44 AM
To SCT

Got it. Totally agree. Something to be aware of and I love your suggestion to say, "OK" and walk away. Also, to notice what energy I give off that says it's OK to criticize me. Xoxo A

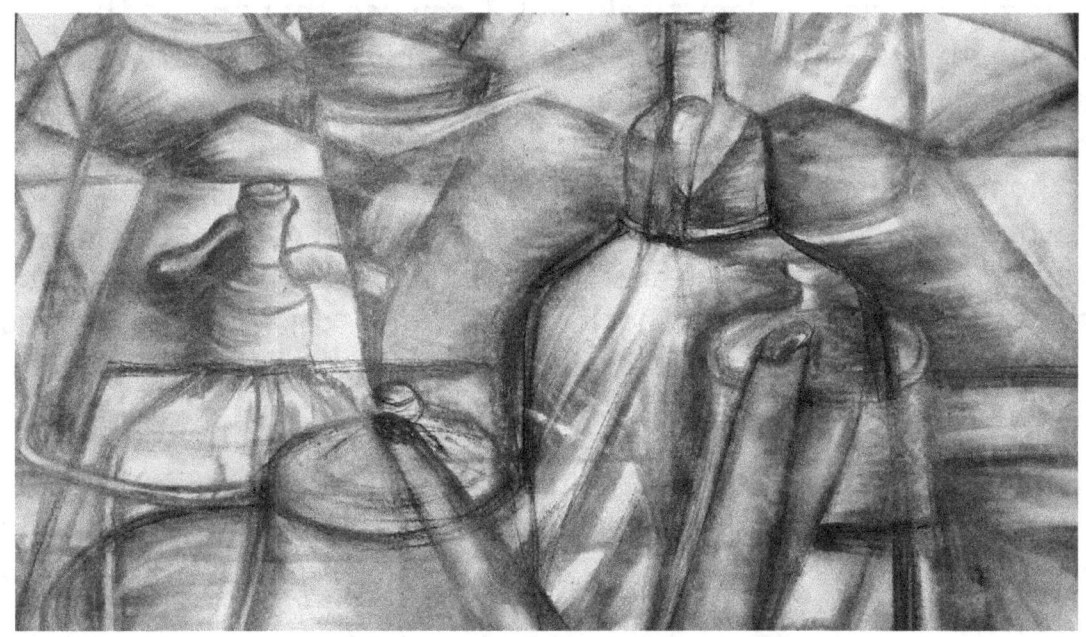

"Still-Life in Black and White"
by Aimee

Advice On Mentees

Aimee:

Now that I have worked with Susan for a number of years, other young women have asked me to be their mentor! This is a major gift to me in my life. Though I am busy, I love getting their calls and I always try to make time for them. Surprisingly, I always seem to get back more than I give!

I feel the deep love and grace of my Higher Power when I pick up the phone and I hear a voice on the other end saying something that I just said myself a few days earlier! And I'm able to respond by saying something that Susan or my homeopath or my minister or my action buddy or trusted friend said to me! It is such a treasure!

I have also seen how this mentoring process, both from Susan and giving to others, has helped me become a better mom to my now-teen and tween girls. They need more from me now on a psychic level, less than on the physical or logistical level. I can see that this is the parenting style I will need to adopt as they move into adulthood. I am a mentor now more than a caregiver. They can feed themselves, get themselves places much of the time, and do their own responsibilities for school and home with much less guidance from me and my husband. It is when they must make difficult choices about friends, school, extracurriculars, or future career/academics that I get to step in and offer my experience, my strength and my hope to them, just as I do with my mentees. I hope to continue mentoring other women throughout my life.

I took classes at the Rhode Island School of Design (RISD) as a child, and for much of my childhood thought I would become a visual artist. In middle school, I realized that I was more in love with dance, music and theatre, and I began to pursue these with greater intensity. Though I still took classes at RISD in high school, visual art was more of a hobby, whereas musical theatre and teaching were going to be more of a career for me. However, throughout my life I have continued to design, draw, paint, collage, and I support my girls in doing the same. It is a form of self-expression and fun for me.

I also was asked to design sets for Imagination Workshop, a non-profit I work with, and have stuck with these endeavors over the years whenever I have been asked. I painted a mural at my daughter's elementary school, collaborating with students and other moms. When I was in college, I was blessed to study abroad in Paris, and I was able to take an art class, painting under the guidance of a fine teacher. I used different media and had a wonderful time creating some artwork which lives in our family cabin in New Hampshire and of which I am proud.

In this book, you will see images of just some of the art I have created over the course of my life. I hope you enjoy the images as much as I have loved creating them!

"Cliff Palace at Sunset"
by Aimee

What Is A God Box?

Aimee:

I have used a God Box for 20 years. It's a place to release one's fears. It's similar to the "Pensieve" in Harry Potter's world where wizards use their magic wands to draw out thoughts that are crowding their brains and minds. These thoughts can then be dropped into a pensieve where they will remain safely until they are able to handle them. The vessel itself is a wide and magicly deep dish made of metal or stone, often elaborately decorated or inlaid with precious stones, and carrying powerful and complex enchantments. Pensieves are rare, because only the most advanced wizards ever use them, and because the majority of wizardkind is afraid of doing so.

For my "Pensieve" or "God Box," I simply write on a piece of paper something that is worrying me, and put it in a pretty box. I write the date, and then I let it go.

It's amazing how many things in that box have worked out over the years, sometimes in unexpected ways! Often, I find that this practice stops me from obsessing about the "problem" and focus on more positive things. This exercise frees my mind to deal with the tasks at hand, and of course, part of my mind usually still addresses the footwork of whatever the issue was. Meanwhile, a Higher Power, I believe, is at work in the background, resolving all things with the best solution for all involved, following nature's plan and spiritual law.

I clean out my God Box years later and marvel at how:

a) I don't remember the issue at all!
b) It has been resolved the way I had hoped
c) It has been resolved in unexpected ways
d) Something better happened, even if I didn't get what I wanted!

The God Box is a wondrous tool for letting go and aligning my will with God's so that I can take my hands off of a problem and not force a solution.

"Still-Life in Orange"
by Aimee

More Gratitudes

AH - Wed, Sept 3. 2014 at 7:17 AM To SCT

1) Remembering to use my God box with all my worries today, and looking through the first several pieces of paper on top I see how each one has already worked out. I guess the box is the right place for them
2) Feeling the weight of responsibility today of running a business and a household, feeling the stress, but knowing that I'm in God's hands and somehow it will all work out
3) Just because I was tired yesterday from my trip doesn't mean I will be tired today
4) A good work day ahead of me - bring the joy
5) Grateful for the cool morning air and my beautiful daughter sitting here eating breakfast and reading to herself

6) It's ok if I don't entertain my kids all the time-they can read while I work and occupy themselves sometimes - they are independent and resilient as a result of some of this necessity - I'm a good enough mom
7) I can bring 80% and do a good enough job as a mom and a worker - my ego tells me I have to be the BEST, but I don't
8) Be of service as I've been taught to do-focus on my mission, not the fear-ask God to remove my fear and direct my attention to what he would have me be

9) How can I keep it simple today? How can I let go? Grateful I've learned to ask these questions and to pray continuously, as continuously as my thoughts come in

love, peace, Aimee

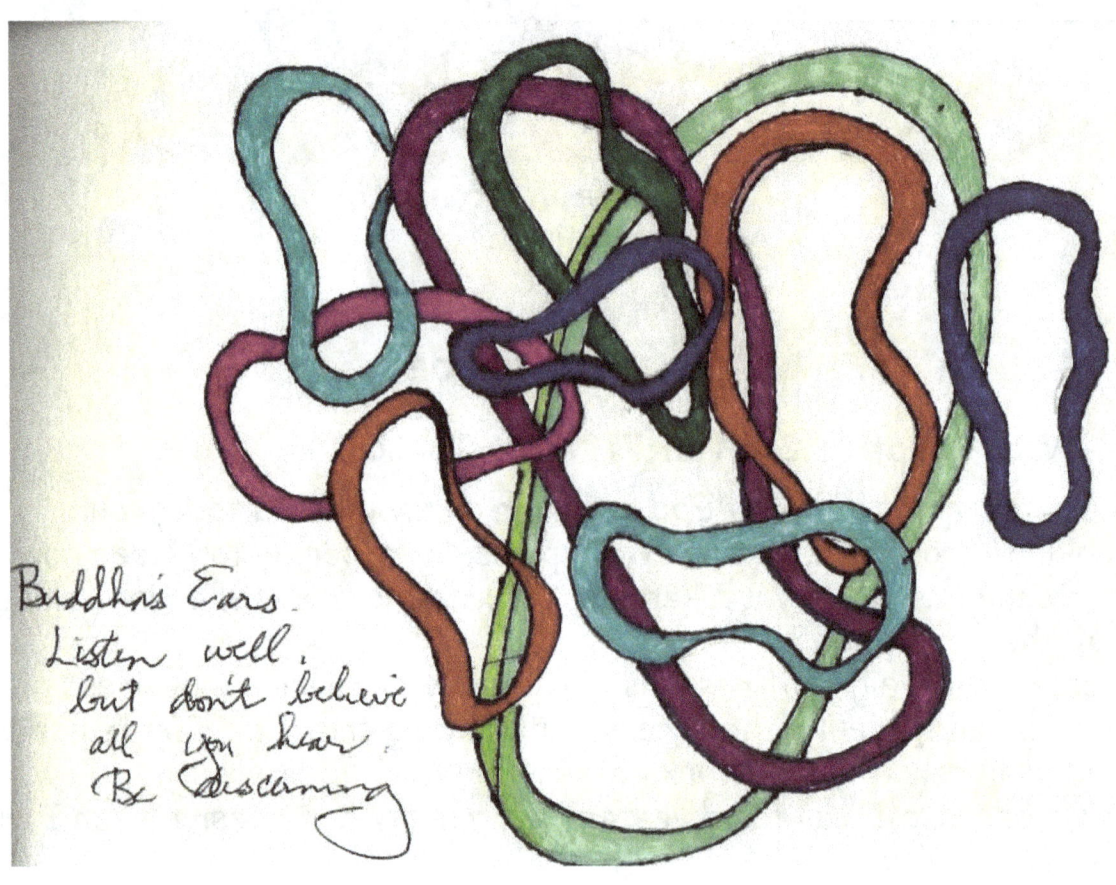

"Buddha's Ears"
by Susan

AH - Fri, Sept. 5, 2014 at 7:22 AM To SCT

1) I'm alive!
2) My life: it's really pretty good, especially when I don't try and hurry it along. Taking care of myself. I need this reminder from Hope For Today - "I am rebuilding my relationship with myself. Self-care is for me, not for others"
3) Finding my groove again after the busiest 3 days in business I can remember - trying to focus on the gratitude and the goodness that my business is growing rather than the overwhelm
4) Learning to ask for help and getting it - from my family, my colleagues, my assistant/bookkeeper - I'm not a "do it all myself and do it all perfectly" person anymore - step 7 has helped me with humility a lot; I'm human, thank God!!!
5) I'm so grateful for my work, I love it, I have great help, and I've learned to manage the stress with the help of friends like you
6) Got childcare for 2 hours so I could clear out emails - thank you!
7) Everyone talks about "it goes so fast" or "I miss when they were little," but I'm also grateful for watching them grow and change and be so successful, great joy in that, and I don't miss the baby years!!! LOL

love, Aimee

SCT - Sat. Sept 6th, 2014 at 1:29 PM To AH

I especially love #1. xxoS

My Gratitudes for Friday and Saturday –

1) Our Little Limpopo River in our garden - love its soothing sound,
2) That Paul and I work through our difficulties and still love each other - easily move through - always know we are the top priority for each other, no matter what happens
3) Getting all the Barbie dolls in the attic washed, mended and dressed to mail to my grand-daughters, Skylar and Bonnie
4) Passing on the young clothes that Georgette made 4 decades ago, keeping them well and now passing them on to our grand-daughters.

Thank you Georgette!! (The paternal grandmother of my two daughters)

AH - Sun, Sept 7, 2014 at 2:11 PM To SCT

1) Though my husband and I work with so many kids and have kids, we have never had head lice, nor have our kids
2) A power outage this am made me shut off screens and do stuff old-style for a while, that was nice
3) I can enjoy peace and quiet so much more now than I used to be able to (I was a "meditation hater" as my friend says!)
4) Time with my spiritual community this am
5) Time hangin' with the kids this afternoon with all the fans on and cold drinks

love, peace, Aimee

AH - Wed - Sept. 10, 2014 at 7:40 AM To SCT

1) Using daughter's Perfect Attendance coupon at Islands last night, dinner for 4, on the cheap, and not having to cook
2) Arriving at work to see that a colleague had set up a PA system for me for my wireless mic (to protect my voice) - unexpected care from others
3) A student bringing me a chair to sit down
4) My daughter writing her own books with invented spelling (I gave the cat a doll uv mick = I gave the cat a bowl of milk)

love, peace, Aimee

SCT - Wed. Sept. 10, 2014 at 9:21 PM To AH

1) Being part of an amazing group of 5 women who get together for an extraordinary evening of dinner, talk and life experiences, sharing every 2 months - it's been 21 years now
2) Being utilized for my expertise at work

3) Driving over Topanga Canyon and seeing/feeling its beauty and wildness
4) Finding benefits of yoga this morning when I didn't get enough sleep and didn't want to go
5) Having yoga students return who were away for the summer
6) Feeling that my life has balance
7) Hearing the successes of my friends and not feeling jealous - just joy!
8) Being a safe haven for a friend who had a big argument with her husband - being non-judgmental
9) Able to be my authentic self most of the time

"Mi Casa es tu Casa"
by Susan

AH - Thursday, Sept 11, 22014 at 6:25 AM To SCT

What a wonderful list! I hope you had a great retreat in Laguna (I think that's where you were) and sounds like you're re- entering in peaceful ways.
love, Aimee

AH - Sat. Sept. 13, 2014 at 7:17 AM To SCT

1) Finally get result of CT-scan - all good
2) Getting drops for my pink eye and seeing ENT about voice - all is well - "You're like Kobe Bryant, sometimes his knee hurts, it's OK - you're a professional!"
3) Ordering tix to a concert for our anniversary Mon, - 13 years
4) Married, 15 years together - a miracle
5) Sending my beautiful kid off to her 1st gym meet today of competition season, doing her hair and eating breakfast with her, packing her gym bag, sending dad off with the video camera
6) My mom and You guys

Xoxo love, Aimee

SCT - Sat. Sept. 13, 2014 at 6:04 PM To AH

Love the Kobe Bryant quote!

1) Went to a birthday party for my high school class - we were all more or less 75! So happy to see faces from so long ago - some difficult to recognize
2) My best friend from 12 years of age - Laurie - still connected at the heart
3) Realizing that all of us still can recall our junior high and high school days-very bonding, enduring and dear
4) Paul agreeing to go with me even though he is bored and neglected - he made his best effort to support me
5) Feeling proud to be my age and also still having an enthusiastic attitude
6) Seeing so many people my age looking great! Maybe they are the ones who come to reunions
7) Feeling happy to recall my teen years no matter what has happened in our lives since then, we all still can see each other at the edge of our adulthood
8) Life always brings me little presents

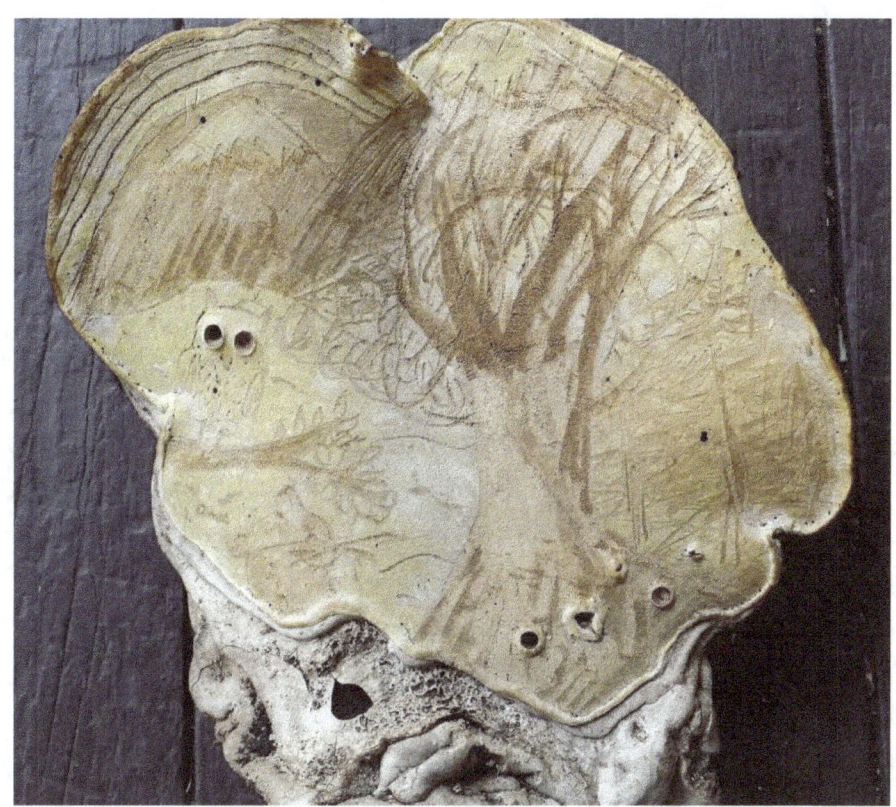

"Owl Eyes"
Fungus carving by Aimee

AH - Sat. Sept. 13, 2014 at 6:04 PM To SCT

1) Time with my girls and husband today just to chill at home with all the fans on Medicine for my eye-feeling better Getting quiet work done-no drama
2) Not freaking out about my voice, just resting, and... amazing! It's better today
3) Peaceful good conversations with other parents dropping off and picking up their kids at our house today - we all have similar struggles, so nice to not be alone
4) A good talk with my mentor yesterday
5) Learning to say no and do things differently - and maybe I'm of service to others by not showing up and possibly passing on germs or having a resentment
6) Learning to take care of myself first, and that doesn't mean I am selfish in a bad way - that's an old tape - I actually have more to give

to others when I don't run around caring for everyone else at my expense, people-pleasing

Love, peace - Aimee

SCT - Sat. Sept. 13, 2014 at 6:04 PM To AH

1) Seeing my husband's spirits unburden since we handled all the "end of life" decisions
2) The kindness of my husband when he realized I didn't sleep well last night - massaging me and listening to me recount my HS years
3) My ability to be truthful and kind
4) Allowing our children to live their own lives without our interference

AH - Mon. Sept. 15, 2014 at 7:17 AM To SCT

1) Surprising and beautiful hearing about my husband going out with my daughter and the whole gym team for ice cream
2) Getting to paint a mural this am at my kids' school with another mom
3) Looking forward to taking my husband out to dinner tonight for our anniversary and surprising him with Elton John concert tix! (shhh...)

Love, peace - Aimee

SCT - Tues, Sept. 16, 2014 at 9:51 PM To AH

1) Seeing my friend Nancy grow as a teacher
2) Having time after yoga to sit on my deck and talk about life with Daedra
3) Having a husband with an easy-going attitude toward all of life
4) Seeing my colleagues, Monk, Keith and Leonardo, do such well-crafted presentations
5) Paul driving so I could do email
6) My growing friendship with Patrice

Unity

This hand gesture — mudra — symbolizes knowledge or wisdom. It calms and focuses the mind and is often used for meditation. As a yoga teacher, I often ask students to think of the forefinger connecting to the thumb as a reminder of their unity with all things; the three other fingers, which are not connected, represent three attitudes, actions or thoughts that are not serving them well. These can be things that are no longer needed, or that are preventing them from releasing emotions and attitudes that have power over their better instincts.

"Unity"
by Susan

I have picked three examples —
- judgements of ourselves or others
- jealousy of things that others have that we want
- competition in terms of besting others to make ourselves seem superior

I certainly could have chosen many others, such as: resentment, non-forgiveness, blame, bullying, exclusion and feelings of superiority. I am sure you can think of more that are relevant to you!

Sometimes, I find that I am only able to select one attitude that I wish to release. Three seems overwhelming. So, I encourage you to start with one and see if you can release its hold over your heart and mind. The idea is to free yourself from thoughts that hold you hostage and take up valuable real estate in both your mind and emotions — and are negatively impacting your health.

Try forming this Mudra as you practice breathing or meditation. Know you are tapping into both your own intuition and into universal wisdom. It is very powerful!

Epilogue

You Can Engage In A More Joyful Life

Susan and Aimee:

Life is a miracle - and, it is mysterious. As long as you are still here, there are new possibilities to explore. Be curious! Explore and discover! Be bold! Listen to what others have to say! Be kind to every person you meet - we are all members of the same human family!

Fully witness and experience our natural world. Add your efforts to care for it. It is filled with awe-inspiring creatures and plants that sustain us. There are natural events and landscapes - as well as variations in weather, landscapes, sunrises and sunsets. Those who study the natural world can get ideas, solve problems, create art - dances, theatre, stories, poetry and music to express their impressions, thoughts and feelings. See connections between what happens in nature and in our own lives. Nature is a library of resources for learning about life on the scientific, mental, emotional and spiritual planes.

Appreciate it all - it is constantly changing and evolving, as are we ourselves. It continues, but doesn't last. The British environmental artist, Andy Goldsworthy, focuses on creating art in nature, using all natural materials. He photographs them when they are completed, but is also interested in seeing how his artwork changes over time and weather conditions. He sees beauty in change. This is a good thought for us to ponder, as well. All of us are born with certain traits, but it is each one of us who creates our life's work. If you can appreciate and accept - even embrace - the changes that occur as we age, then your work of art will always be of value.

"Swiss Chateau in Oberhofen"
by Aimee

Prompts

Susan and Aimee:

Here are some things you can do to activate your desire and ability to find gratitude in each day.

1. Write down all the physical aspects of your health that you can identify. Do this even if you are challenged by discomfort, a handicap or illness. Think of all of the things that are going right rather than all that is wrong. It will begin to make a difference in your attitude and mood - and this can be the best medicine for increasing your health and well being.

No matter the state of your health, begin with gratitude for the experience of being alive. Life is a miracle. Life is a mystery. You have been given a chance to see, hear, feel, do, think about and experience many things. Take a moment to thank each aspect of your body for allowing you to participate in life.

2. Write down one or two things you would like to improve in terms of your health. Remember that so much begins with a positive and hopeful attitude. Change happens moment to moment - it is a constant and is always possible. In every moment there are possibilities to make new choices and take new actions.

3. Think of a person for whom you are grateful. Then, write down all the qualities about that person that you appreciate.

4. Think of people with whom you do not agree nor enjoy your interactions together. Rather than writing down everything you don't like about them, think of their admirable traits. (You don't have to like them!) This may not convert them from enemies to friends, but it can bring balance to your own life. It is the negative feelings that we often cling to so tightly that are more destructive than the actual people who trigger our negative emotions. (Start with just one person!)

5. Write down all the qualities you like about yourself - only positive ones, nothing negative. Thank yourself for making choices that have led to you becoming the person you are. Whatever your current state of being, see the goodness within yourself. Giving gratitude for these positive traits will strengthen your ability to decide who you really wish to be - adding, rather than subtracting from the universal field of energy.

6. Think of just one positive quality you would like to strengthen within yourself. Here are a few samples: kindness; clear focus; respectful listening; courage to do right; showing appreciation; supporting others; moving from fear to curiosity; contributing to the environment; consistency; determination; meditation; walking and observing nature; etc.

7. List 10 things you are grateful for in your life. Do this for 1 week. Don't read your lists until the end of the last day. See what themes stand out. Are there any limitations? What have you repeated? Can you stretch your thinking to include a wider span of things in your life - things that perhaps you haven't thought of before?

Note: If you wish, write 10 more things each day for another week. Review your lists at the end of the last day and see if any changes occurred. Are there any themes emerging? Are there areas of your life that are unacknowledged?

8. If you want to take your gratitudes further, it is a powerful experience to ask an interested friend to join you in both writing and sharing daily, or weekly, gratitudes.

9. Here is a mantra - an affirmation - I designed for myself. I say it daily. If it resonates with you, then please use it and see if you feel more validated in these three aspects of living your life.

> "I will always BE enough.
> I will always HAVE enough.
> I will always DO enough."

This helps to keep me in "gratitude mode" and to realize that when I feel unaccomplished in any of these three areas of Being, it returns me to balance and contentment.

If I start to doubt myself or feel that there will never be enough to sustain, or satisfy me, I repeat this mantra several times - or even several times a day. It is also a wonderful antidote to feelings of jealousy, competition, low self-esteem and self-judgment!

We hope that our experience in changing our attitude from what's missing to what's here will help you do the same. Begin your day with gratitude that you are still here, that you have the potential to make your life more joyful.

almost
THE END

"Home Office of Beauty and the Beast"
by Aimee

List Of Artwork

"The Enchanted Castle" painting by Aimee. . . . . Cover
"Ten Past Toucan" collage by Susan . . . . Page 5
"Randolph Rainbows" carving by Aimee. . . . . Page 6
"What Goes Around Comes Around" collage by Susan . . . . . Page 7
"Fruit in a Blue Bowl" by Susan . . . . Page 9
"We Shared Something" collage by Susan . . . . Page 10
"Childhood Home" by Aimee . . . . Page 11
"Twilight at the Café de la Créativité" by Aimee . . . . Page 13
"Artist Kim's Studio #1" by Susan . . . . Page 15
"Artist Kim Studio #2" by Susan. . . . . Page 18
"Under My Hat" by Susan. Page 19
"Shared Dreams" collage by Susan . . . . Page 20
"Sunset with Beach Grass" by Aimee. . . . . Page 21
"Jealousy Has a Long Red Tongue" by Susan. . . . . Page 22
Vision Board by Aimee . . . . Page 24
"Ravine House Raft" by Aimee . . . . Page 27
"The Divine Feminine" by Aimee . . . . Page 29
"Joy" by Susan . . . . Page 30
"Determined Pachyderm" by Susan . . . . Page 30
"View from Mountain Porch" by Aimee . . . . Page 33
"Sunflower Tea" by Susan . . . . Page 35
"Banana Leaves" by Susan . . . . Page 37
"Bumpy Car Ride to Cashel & Tipperary" by Susan . . . . . . Page 39
"Squared Spirals" by Susan . . . . Page 41
"Yin and Yang—a Constant Struggle for Balance" by Susan . . Page 42
"Lupe's Mother's Day Gift" by Susan . . . . Page 43
Another Example of a Vision Board by Aimee . . . . Page 48
"The Tree that Blooms" by Susan . . . . Page 49
"Laguna Beach" by Susan . . . . Page 52
"Floating Market, Thailand" by Susan . . . . Page 53
"Red & Green Leaves" drawing by Susan . . . . Page 56
"Create Beauty" by Susan . . . . Page 58
"Kauai #1" by Susan . . . . Page 60
"Life Cycles" collage by Susan . . . . Page 62
"Hundred Acre Cove" by Aimee . . . . Page 64
"Aging" collage by Susan . . . . Page 66
"Greeting Each Moment" collage by Susan . . . . Page 67

"The Tree of Insight" by Susan . . . . Page 72
"Aimee Self-Portrait in Paris" by Aimee . . . . Page 74
"New Hampshire Sunset" by Aimee . . . . Page 76
"Barrington Harbor" by Aimee . . . . Page 77
"Creative Light Bulb" by Susan . . . . Page 79
"Still-Life in Black and White" by Aimee . . . . Page 81
"Cliff Palace at Sunset" by Aimee . . . . Page 83
"Still-Life in Orange" by Aimee . . . . Page 85
"Buddha's Ears" by Susan . . . . Page 86
"Mi Casa es tu Casa" collage by Susan . . . . Page 89
"Owl eyes" carving by Aimee . . . . Page 91
"Unity" by Susan . . . . Page 93
"Swiss Chateau in Oberhofen" by Aimee . . . . Page 95
"Home Office of Beauty and the Beast" by Aimee. . . . . . . Page 98

THE END!

www.ingramcontent.com/pod-product-compliance
Lightning Source LLC
Chambersburg PA
CBHW081156070526
44583CB00021B/2866